TEACHING TO CHANGE LIVES

TEACHING TO Change LIVES

MULTNOMAH PUBLISHERS, INC.
SISTERS, OREGON

DR. HOWARD HENDRICKS

TEACHING TO CHANGE LIVES

published by Multnomah Publishers, Inc.

© 1987 by Multnomah Press

International Standard Book Number: 0-88070-969-3
(previously 0-88070-271-0)

Cover design by Kevin Keller

Lesson Plans by Miles Lewis, Ed. D.

Printed in the United States of America

Quotations from John Milton Gregory's
The Seven Laws of Teaching (first published in 1884)
are from the 1917 edition revised by
William C. Bagley and Warren K. Layton,
and reprinted by Baker Book House in 1954.

Most Scripture quotations are from:

The Holy Bible, New International Version (NIV)
© 1973, 1984 by International Bible Society,
used by permission of Zondervan Publishing House

Other Scripture quotations are from:

The New Testament in Modern English,
Revised Edition (Phillips) © 1972 by J. B. Phillips

and the author's own translation

This book is co-published by Walk Through the Bible
Ministries under the title The Seven Laws of the Teacher.

For information:
MULTNOMAH PUBLISHERS, INC.
POST OFFICE BOX 1720
SISTERS, OREGON 97759

Library of Congress Cataloging-in-Publication Data:

Hendricks, Howard G.
Teaching to change lives.
1. Christian education—Teaching methods.
2. Teaching—Religious aspects—Christianity.
3. Hendricks, Howard G.   I. Title.
BV1534.H44   1987   268'.6   87-11208

02 03 04 05   29 28 27

To My Students

my most inquisitive teachers,

my most persistent challenge,

my most enduring fulfillment

We continually remember
before our God and Father
your work produced by faith,
your labor prompted by love,
and your endurance inspired by
hope in our Lord Jesus Christ.
1 Thessalonians 1:3

Contents

FOREWORD

Howard Hendricks.

Within evangelical educational circles, the very name means "Christian Education." Not only has Dr. Hendricks been in the forefront of the modern Christian education movement, but he is a forceful and dynamic Bible teacher whose messages result in changed lives. But more than that for me personally, he's a great friend and challenging mentor.

Our relationship began when I was a student in seminary, and I was captured by the dynamic learning experiences in his classes. Frankly, I "majored" in Howard Hendricks!

Why did I and so many, many other students take every class we possibly could from this one man? Because he cared. He cared about each one of us as individuals and as future communicators. He cared about the truths we would learn in his classes. He cared about the whole process of excellent communication. Yes, he cared about us, and it showed in every word he spoke and every movement he made. The fact is, he was not so much teaching a course as he was ministering to his students.

That's why, when I did my master's thesis on using revolutionary teaching methods in presenting an overview of the Old Testament, I relied on Dr. Hendricks as my adviser. And that's why, when we launched Walk Thru the Bible Ministries as an outgrowth of that thesis, I asked Dr. Hendricks to serve on our board of directors. He continues to inspire and challenge me in that crucial role.

You see, every class Dr. Hendricks taught in my four years in seminary was so motivating and helpful that we students used to think that, by the time we were seniors, just maybe once he would be boring. "Maybe today he'll lay an egg," we'd josh with one another. Well, we're still waiting.

Toward the end of my final year in seminary, I decided to test Prof Hendricks. I came into the classroom, sat in the back row, and determined not to pay attention. I just looked out the window into the parking lot. I was going to time him to see how long he could cope with a student who wasn't with him.

Well, Prof had a routine in starting every class. He sat behind his desk, and you could watch his leg start bouncing about three minutes before the class started, as if he were getting wound up and ready to go. At the stroke of the hour, he would open his mouth and start speaking. And we were off. And he'd sit there for about eight minutes, teaching. At that point, he'd get up from his chair, go to the board, and draw a great chart. Then he'd tell a pertinent joke and go on with his outline.

This day, I just looked out the window. And he was out from behind his desk in under one minute. He was drawing terrific charts on the board, and I was doing my best not to copy them down. Then he started telling jokes. Lots of jokes. And I tried my hardest to keep from laughing. Then he moved to the corner of the room, directly in my path, gesturing wildly. But still I stared out the window.

At the three-minute-thirty-seven-second mark, he was running down the aisle toward me, screaming, "Wilkinson! What on earth are you looking at?" So I apologized and started paying attention. And I didn't tell him about my little experiment until years later.

You see, Dr. Hendricks was so committed to seeing his students learn that it drove him to distraction if he was failing in that commitment. And he would do whatever it took to get that one student back on track in the learning process. That's dedication. No, that's *teaching*. But, frankly, it's a kind of teaching we don't see much of these days.

In schools, churches, sanctuaries, seminars—whatever the teaching situation may be, the name of the game these days seems not to be teaching, but covering material. And as a result, we see unmotivated students who, rather than be engrossed by the lesson and enjoy it, merely endure it…at best. Students who couldn't care less about how the truths they've been exposed to can change their lives.

Because you've picked up this book, that tells me you're the kind of teacher who wants to continue growing in order to see the lives of your students blossom and flourish as God intended.

If that's true, then you've picked up the right book. Because for the first time, Dr. Hendricks has distilled his decades of expertise on the subject of communication into seven practical laws—"The Seven Laws of the Teacher." They're designed just for you—to help you generate even greater impact in the lives of those you teach.

This book is just one part of a series of life-changing practical insights for communicators presented in a video and live seminar series we've called "The Applied Principles of Learning,"™ or "APL" for short. Dr. Hendricks's seven laws have been captured on videotape just as he presented them before an audience of hundreds of teachers from around the country—people just like you who wanted to improve their teaching skills.

These seven videotapes, which also feature dramatic vignettes, are available for purchase by your church or school group from Walk Thru the Bible Ministries. Along with this book, a colorful course notebook is also available to help you record your notes and insights as you view the videos, as well as encourage you through practical exercises to put the laws you learn to work in your own teaching situations. A leader's guide for group facilitation can also be used to get maximum benefit from this series.

My part of the Applied Principles of Learning series, complementing Dr. Hendricks's laws, is called "The Seven Laws of the Learner." My live seminars are offered on videotape as a companion course to his, with a course notebook, textbook, and leader's guide. I know you'll benefit from either series, whether you are using the videotaped sessions or simply reading the book.

You can use Dr. Hendricks's video series on your own, or as part of a teacher training program in your church or school. Watch each session once a week for seven weeks, or schedule a weekend teachers' retreat. Be sure to use the workbook materials to help you understand the law personally and apply it to your own teaching. This book can then serve as a refresher to Dr. Hendricks's video lessons—a source you can turn to time and time again to nail down these exciting biblical truths in your own life.

Let me assure you, when you start practicing the laws presented in the APL series, you'll find your teaching to be far more exciting and fulfilling than you ever thought possible, because you'll see life-change in your students.

That's what happened to me as I sat under the teaching of this man in a seminary classroom. And it can happen to you too as you turn the page, or flip on your video monitor, and listen to Dr. Hendricks share his insights with you. The result, my friend, will be truly revolutionary.

BRUCE H. WILKINSON
President & Founder
Walk Thru the Bible Ministries, Inc.
Atlanta, Georgia

A Passion to Communicate

With the kind of start I had in life, I'm sure I could have soon died and gone to hell and nobody would have particularly cared. I was born into a broken home, my parents having separated before I was born. The only time I ever saw them together was eighteen years later when I was called to testify in a divorce court.

As a boy I lived in a neighborhood in north Philadelphia in which they said an evangelical church could never be planted. But God has a fantastic sense of humor whenever anyone decides what can't be done. He led a small group of Christians to band together, buy a little house there, and start a church.

One man in the church was named Walt. He had only a sixth-grade education. One day Walt told the Sunday school superintendent he wanted to start a Sunday school class. "That's great, Walt," he was told, "but we don't have an opening for you." Walt insisted, however, so the superintendent said, "Good. Go out and get a class. Anybody you find is yours."

Then Walt came into my community. The first time we met I was playing marbles out on the concrete. "Son," he said, "how would you like to go to Sunday school?"

I wasn't interested. Anything with school in it had to be bad news.

So he said, "How about a game of marbles?"

That was different. So we shot marbles and had a great time, though he whipped me in every single game. (Now you know: I lost my marbles early in life.) By then I would have followed him anywhere.

Walt picked up a total of thirteen boys in that community for his Sunday school class, of whom nine were from broken homes. Eleven of the thirteen are now in full-time vocational Christian work.

Actually, I can't tell you much of what Walt said to us, but I can tell you everything about him…because he loved me for Christ's sake. He loved me more than my parents did.

He used to take us hiking, and I'll never forget those times. I'm sure we made his bad heart worse, but he'd run all over those woods with us because he cared.

He was not the most scintillating person in the world, but he was for real. I knew it, and so did everyone else in that class.

So you see, my interest in teaching is much more than professional. It's also intensely personal—and, in fact, a passion—because the only reason I have a ministry today is that God brought along my path a committed teacher.

This book is about seven strategic concepts in teaching, and you'll notice we're calling them "laws"—principles, rules.

The Law of the Teacher
The Law of   Education
The Law of   Activity
The Law of   Communication
The Law of the Heart
The Law of   Encouragement
The Law of   Readiness

If you boil them all down, these seven laws essentially call *for a passion to communicate.*

Years ago I took part in a Sunday school convention at Moody Memorial Church in Chicago. During a lunch break, three of us who were teaching at the convention walked across the street to a little hamburger shop. The place was filled, but soon a table for four opened up. We saw an elderly lady whom we knew was attending the convention because of the bag she was carrying, and we asked her to join us.

We learned she was eighty-three and from a town in Michigan's Upper Peninsula. In a church with a Sunday school of only sixty-five people, she taught a class of thirteen junior-high boys. She had traveled by Greyhound bus all the way to Chicago the night before the convention. Why? In her words, "To learn something that would make me a better teacher."

I thought at the time, "Most people who had a class of thirteen junior-high boys in a Sunday school of only sixty-five would be breaking their arms to pat themselves on the back: 'Who, me? Go to a Sunday school convention? I could teach it myself!' " But not this woman.

Eighty-four boys who sat under her teaching are now young men in full-time vocational ministry. Twenty-two are graduates of the seminary where I teach.

If you were to ask me the secret to this woman's impact, I'd give you a totally different answer today from what I would have said thirty years ago. Back then I'd have credited her methodology.

Now I believe it was because of her passion to communicate.

My heart's concern for you is that God will give you a passion like that...and never let it die.

And I hope you never get over the thrill that someone will actually listen to you and learn from you.

The

teacher must know that

which he would teach....

Imperfect knowing

must be reflected in

imperfect teaching.

John Milton Gregory

1

THE LAW OF THE TEACHER

The effective teacher always teaches from the overflow of a full life.

The Law of the Teacher, simply stated, is this: *If you stop growing today, you stop teaching tomorrow.*

Neither personality nor methodology can substitute for this principle. You cannot communicate out of a vacuum. You cannot impart what you do not possess. If you don't know it—truly know it— you can't give it.

This law embraces the philosophy that I, as a teacher, am primarily a learner, a student among students. I am perpetuating the learning process; I am still en route. And by becoming a student again, I as a teacher will look at the education process through a radically new—and uniquely personal— set of eyes.

I must keep growing and changing. The word of God, of course, does not change, but my understanding of it does change, because I am a developing individual. This is why Peter could tell us at the end of his second epistle, *"Grow* in the grace and knowledge of our Lord and Savior Jesus Christ."

Such a philosophy requires a certain attitude—the attitude that you have not yet "arrived." A person who applies this principle of teaching is always asking, "How can I improve?"

Think of it this way: As long as you live, you learn; and as long as you learn, you live.

When I was a college student—back before the earth's crust hardened— I worked in the college dining hall, and on my way to work at 5:30 every morning I walked past the home of one of my professors. Through a window I could see the light on at his desk, morning after morning.

At night I stayed late at the library to take advantage of evening study hours, and returning home at 10:30 or 11 o'clock, I would again see his desk light on. He was always poring over his books.

One day he invited me home for lunch, and after the meal I said to him, "Would you mind if I asked you a question?"

"Of course not."

"What keeps you studying? You never seem to stop."

His answer, I learned later, was in the words of another—but they had become his own: "Son, I would rather have my students drink from a running stream than a stagnant pool."

He was one of the best professors I ever had—a man who marked me permanently.

How about those you teach? From what are they drinking?

Let me challenge you with a statement in Luke 6, from the last part of verse 40: "Everyone who is fully trained will be like his teacher."

People tell me they can't believe Jesus said that. In all the years they've been reading the gospels, they never noticed it. But now it motivates them to ask God to change their lives by his grace—and to change it drastically. How about you? Does that principle in Luke 6:40 represent an exciting prospect to you—or a frightening one?

No matter how it makes you feel, if you want to minister to others, ask God first of all to minister to you. He wants to work through you, but he can't until he works *in* you. He'll use you as his instrument, but he wants to sharpen and cleanse that instrument so it becomes a more effective tool in his hands.

All this is true because *human personality* is the vehicle of effective teaching.

Don't ask me to explain that. I'm just thankful to God I can experience it. I've long been convinced God could have used far more efficient instruments than you or me to get this job done; nevertheless, he's chosen to work through us. Most of us can accept that only by faith. But it's true. The miracle of the ministry is that God handpicked us to be his representatives to this generation. He wants to bring about change, and in doing it, *you* will be one of his critical instruments. How does that grab you?

So if you want to strengthen your teaching—and that's obviously why you're reading this book—then do everything in your power to strengthen the teacher—yourself.

I want to help you do that.

The Search for Teachers

Years ago, a cartoon showed two frames, each with a Mr. Brown talking with a young woman in his office.

In the first frame he's a public school superintendent, and he says, "I'm awfully sorry, Miss Smith, but after reviewing your application for a teaching position, we've decided we can't use you. We must have someone with at least five years' experience in teaching and preferably with a master's degree in education."

In the second frame Mr. Brown is a Sunday school superintendent, and he says, "You'd make a *wonderful* teacher, Miss Smith. I realize you haven't been a Christian very long, and you feel you don't know much about the Bible—but there's no finer way to learn the Bible than to teach it. And you say you have no experience working with kids in this age group—but I'm convinced you'll grow to understand and love them. Really, Miss Smith, all we're looking for is a willing heart."

What a sad but true commentary on our low regard for the teaching of God's word. To teach children that two plus two equals four, you need a minimum of four years of higher education. To teach the unsearchable riches of Jesus Christ, anything is good enough…and that's why it too often degenerates into a ministry of mediocrity.

In the search for good teachers, I always look for FAT people—those who are Faithful, Available, and Teachable.

What they know in their heads is not the determining factor. But are they faithful in what they have done? Are they available to teach—without arm-twisting? And are they willing to learn?

In many of our Sunday schools we're discovering that we get the largest number of committed teachers simply by getting them gradually involved in the process. Then they get hooked. They come to look in on the programs for high schoolers, for example. And hanging around those teenagers really sells them on the idea that (1) they can have a ministry in these kids' lives, and (2) it's a very rewarding investment.

Most adults are initially afraid to become involved because their confidence level is so low. Our task is to build them up, and with a little time and involvement, it can be done.

In passing, I'll also say that if I were responsible for selecting a Sunday school teaching staff, I would immediately eliminate three things:

First, all public announcements of this sort: *"Beloved!* Won't you PLEASE teach in our Sunday school? We've been trying for WEEKS to get more teachers and NO ONE will help!"

Second, all arm-twisting. "Change your mind and teach for us, whaddya say? Takes no time at all. We've got a quarterly teacher's guide. You can read, can't you? If you can read it, you can teach it, so give it a try, okay?"

Third, all last-minute appointments. The panicky Sunday school superintendent rushes into the adult class on the first Sunday morning of the quarter, grabs the closest guy sitting on the end of the row, and sentences him for life to teach in the junior department. The moral of which is, Don't sit on the end of the row.

Making Change

If you would, please grab a pen and write down somewhere in the margins on this page your answer to this question: How have you changed...*lately?* In the last week? Or the last month? The last year?

Can you be *very specific?* Or must your answer be incredibly vague?

You say you're growing. Okay...how? "Well," you say, "in all kinds of ways." Great! Name *one.*

You see, effective teaching comes only through a changed person. The more you change, the more you become an instrument of change in the lives of others.

If you want to become a change agent, *you* also must change.

Allow me to draw your life. If the arrows of your life—your frontiers, your questions, your interests, your mental energies—move this way...

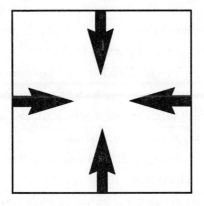

you are in the process of dying. But if the arrows in your life are moving in these directions...

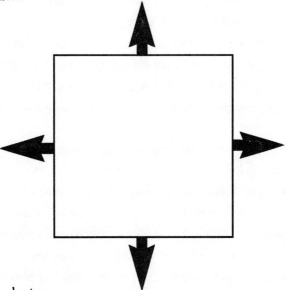

then you're developing.

This has nothing to do with your age, incidentally—and everything to do with your attitude.

I'm so tired of running into people who say, "Well, Brother Hendricks, I'm just getting too old."

"How old is too old?" I ask. "Have you died?"

"Oh, no, no, I'm still alive."

"Good. Then learn—or else you will slowly die mentally. And then you may as well lie down and we'll put you in the box."

Older people can be excellent learners, but frequently they are conditioned against learning. Somewhere along the line they were infected with the idea that you can't teach an old dog new tricks—which is true, if you're teaching dogs, and if you're teaching tricks.

But you and I are not in the business of either one. We're teaching people, and we're teaching truth.

Some of the most exciting and fulfilled people you'll ever meet are older people who have decided *not* to stop learning. I know students in their twenties who are dead in the head. Yet I have friends who are sixty-five or seventy-five or eighty-five and very much alive.

I brought one into my seminary class awhile ago, a man ninety-three who had been saved and serving Christ for eighty-four of those years. He told the students, "As far as I'm concerned, my only regret is that I have only one life to give in service to Jesus Christ." The class gave him a six-minute, standing ovation.

Some time ago I lost one of my best friends, a woman eighty-six years old, the most exciting lay teacher I've ever been exposed to.

The last time I saw her on planet Earth was at one of those aseptic Christian parties. We were sitting there on eggshells, looking pious, when she walked in and said, "Well, Hendricks, I haven't seen you for a long time. What are the five best books you've read in the past year?"

She had a way of changing a group's dynamics. Her philosophy was, Let's not bore each other with each other; let's get into a discussion, and if we can't find anything to discuss, let's get into an argument.

She was eighty-three on her last trip to the Holy Land. She went there with a group of NFL football players. One of my most vivid memories of her is seeing her out front yelling back to them, "Come on, men, get with it!"

She died in her sleep at her daughter's home in Dallas. Her daughter told me that just before she died, she had written out her goals for the next ten years.

May her tribe increase!

The apostle Paul is another example. Near the end of his life, at a time when most people are looking for rocking chairs, he said, "Forgetting what is behind and straining toward what is ahead, *I press on* toward the goal to win the prize for which God has called me heavenward in Christ Jesus" (Philippians 3:13–14, italics mine).

Look at that passage carefully, and you'll see that Paul was properly related to the past—neither enamored of his successes nor defeated by his failures. You learn from the past, but you don't live in it.

He was also properly related to the future. Here lay his goal, his hope.

And he was just as properly related to the present. Here and now, he said, "I press on." He was grabbing the challenge.

How many people in our churches, at an age when they ought to be tearing the world apart, are instead sliding home?

Of course, as you get older like me, it can get harder to remember things you're learning because you get ants in your attic. Jeanne and I have been memorizing Psalms. Sometimes I'll ask her, "Can you give me Psalm 40?" She repeats it, and I'll say, "Wonderful, Sweetheart, but you forgot verse seven."

Then she'll have me say it, and when I'm through, she responds, "Howie, you're making tremendous progress. But you forgot verses four to sixteen."

Growth: The Larger Picture

The most exciting thing about working with some of the new converts I've known is that the moment they understand something from God's word, they rush out the door to put it into practice.

You see, they haven't been around long enough to learn all the games we older Christians play. We have so many ways to waltz around the truth. When we run into something over which we do not care to change our lives, we explain it away. Such as, "Well, that refers to the Jews." It's amazing how much we dump on those dear people.

To strengthen your own commitment to change and development, remember that growing is something even the Lord Jesus did. Luke 2:52 explains the developmental process in his life: "Jesus *grew*," we are told, in four areas:

He grew "in wisdom." That's intellectual development.

He grew "in stature"—physical development.

He grew "in favor with God"—spiritual development.

And he grew "in favor with men"—social and emotional development.

Please note that spiritual development is *a part of the larger process*. It can't be our sole concern. Spiritual growth should not be compartmentalized, but integrated with every other aspect of life.

This is where we've been missing it.

As a professor at a theological seminary, I teach some of the most sincerely and highly motivated students in all the world—young men and women climbing the heights with commitment. They are not in the business of playing games.

Yet strangely enough, many of them have never been helped to understand that they cannot fully develop spiritually unless they develop in life's other areas as well—intellectually, physically, socially, and emotionally. You cannot neglect one of these areas without endangering your growth in all of them. Likewise, you cannot grow in any one of these areas without also having an effect on all the others.

So don't limit Jesus Christ to some religious compartment and say, "A chapter a day keeps the devil away." Wake up to the realization that each day you can give the Lord of your life even greater control over every aspect of your being. This is what makes the Christian life dynamic and not static. This is what keeps your fizz from going flat.

But please note at the outset that this is a highly individualized process. We all come from different backgrounds and are in different stages of development in our Christian life. That's why comparison is carnality. Don't spend your time comparing yourself with him or with her, because you're not them. You are *you*.

So go back to the drawing board, and for each major area of your life ask yourself, "Lord, how am I doing?"

In some of these battlefields of growth you'll show up very well, and you're demonstrating giant steps of improvement. In others you're going to show up rather poorly, and you have a long way to go.

You'll discover that some of your values and habits need to be *retained*.

Some of them need to be *refined*.

And some of them need to be *rejected* outright.

But we're all in the same boat, because we're all *in process*.

And in that process, how wonderful it is to ask, "Am I doing the right things?" One of the greatest fears I have for my students after graduation is not that they will fail, but that they will succeed at doing the wrong things— that they'll reach the end of the line and discover that this isn't the destination they wanted, and it can't fulfill them.

I've been involved in a ministry to professional athletes, and something each one of them must face up to is that he can make a mountain of money and have tremendous influence and women throwing themselves at his feet—and yet never come to grips with who he really is. Is there life after football? Or do you just end up with a nice collection of trophies and a drawer full of sports-page clippings? There's nothing staler than an old athlete.

Your Intellectual Dimension

Let me give you three suggestions for growing in the intellectual dimension of your life.

1. *Maintain a consistent study and reading program.* Understand that leaders are readers, and readers are leaders.

But I find a lot of people who say, "You know, Dr. Hendricks, I'm reading a lot of things, but frankly I'm not finding that it changes my life or contributes that much."

Here's a way out: If you have an hour set apart to read, try reading the first half-hour and use the second half-hour to *reflect* on what you read. Watch the difference it makes. You're reading too much if you reflect on it too little.

And get involved not only in reading books, but in reading people as well. The two factors that will influence you the most in the years ahead are the books you read and the people you're around.

People are stimulating—and you'll find it easier to get involved with them as you experience more of the sheer fascination of it.

One of the greatest lessons my father taught me was this: Whenever you're around a significant person, keep your mouth shut except to ask penetrating questions. If you're with those who know more than you know, pick their brains and take advantage of what they have. Let them do the talking and tell you everything they know.

I never cease to be amazed how seldom we make the best use of a resource individual. I've been flown all across America and paid a consultant's fee, only to sit with a group who spend the bulk of their time arguing with each other.

2. *Enroll in continuing education courses*—courses that will improve not only your content, but also your skill. Today there are more good opportunities of this kind to enrich your mind and develop your gifts than ever before.

But the most important course is your own personal Bible study program. In all my years I've never found a layperson with a significant spiritual ministry who does not also have a strong personal intake of God's word.

Many of us who are "under" the word of God are not "in" it for ourselves—getting into it and letting it get into us. A woman once told me, "Dr. Hendricks, I've been through the Bible twenty-nine times." "Wonderful, Madam," I answered. "And how many times has the Bible been through you?"

When the word of God is at the heart of a teaching ministry, no one alive can fully imagine the impact it can have. Paul gives us refreshing insight into this in 2 Timothy 2:2. He's telling Timothy, "I communicated to you the body of truth I received by revelation, and with it I built truth into your life. Now I'm charging you to take that same truth and deposit it into the lives of other reliable individuals, teaching them in such a way that they'll be equipped to teach others…who'll teach others…who'll teach others."

It's a ministry of *multiplication*. Every time you teach you launch a process that ideally will never end, generation after generation.

3. *Get to know your students.* Become an authority on the needs and general characteristics of their age group. But go beyond that; get to your students individually. Find out as much about them as you possibly can.

Years ago in a church in Dallas we were having trouble finding a teacher for a junior-high boys class. The list of prospects had only one name—and when they told me who it was, I said, "You've got to be kidding." But I couldn't have been more wrong about that young man. He took the class and revolutionized it.

I was so impressed I invited him to my home for lunch and asked him the secret of his success. He pulled out a little black book. On each page he had a small picture of one of the boys, and under the boy's name were comments like "having trouble in arithmetic," or "comes to church against parents' wishes," or "would like to be a missionary some day but doesn't think he has what it takes."

"I pray over those pages every day," he said, "and I can hardly wait to come to church each Sunday to see what God has been doing in their lives."

I challenge you to pray over your students this way—whether they're nursery kids or senior citizens. But let me give you a warning that comes from too much experience: As we work with people, always remember that labels are libel. So often we label our students—"she never talks," "he's the trou- blemaker," and so on. Never hang a label like that around someone's neck.

In the fifth grade in public school I had a teacher named Miss Simon. I'll never forget Miss Simon…and I doubt Miss Simon ever forgot me. When I told her my name on the first day of class, she said, "Oh—Howard Hendricks. I've heard a lot about you. I understand you're the worst kid in this school."

"What a challenge," I thought. "If she thinks I'm the worst kid in the school, I guarantee I'll never slip into second place!" And I didn't disappoint her.

Sometimes I ask teachers, "Which kids in your class do you like the most?" And they'll say, "Oh, there's a pretty little girl with long curls, and she never peeps, never gives me any problems." Well, she may still not be peeping twenty years from now. But the kid who's climbing the walls today may become your pastor or a missionary tomorrow. Kids with enough creative energy to get into trouble can have enough drive to live highly significant lives for Jesus Christ later on. Sometimes they come into our Sunday school class so energetic and excited and curious, and what do we do? We whip it all out of them: "*Hey, cut that out! Don't you know this is Sunday school?*"

Your Physical Dimension

Is there anything in the physical dimension of your life over which, in obedience to Christ, you do not have proper control?

Ouch! The physical dimension is often the area evangelical Christians neglect most consistently. The reason: We're prone to deny our humanity. So we're forever prostituting the body, even though there's as much hope for your body as there is for your soul. The Bible is so full of this teaching it's a wonder we escape it. (By the way, if you want to know the greatest areas of need in your Christian life, try looking sometime at passages you have *not* underlined in your Bible.)

We talk a lot about being filled by the Holy Spirit, so it's fascinating to see in what areas of our lives we tend to apply that concept—and what areas we consistently avoid.

Allow me to get personal. Is your money under control? Most Christian financial counselors will tell you firsthand we're out to lunch in this area. Did you know that 80 percent of all Americans owe more than their net worth? And yet an incredible amount of money passes through our hands. American Christians especially will have a lot to give an account for when they get to the judgment seat of Christ, because to whom much has been given, much will be required.

What about your material possessions? My wife Jeanne and I once dined with a rich man from a blue blood Boston family, and I asked him, "How in the world did you grow up in the midst of such wealth and not be consumed by materialism?"

His answer: "My parents taught us that everything in our home was either an idol or a tool."

So how do you view your possessions?

And how about your use of time? Do you have control there? Because if you don't control it, someone else will—someone who doesn't have your priority system. Everywhere I go I find people who have a wonderful plan for my life, and they're usually telling me it's God's plan as well.

Is your sex life under control, living as we are in a cesspool society? So many people have never let Jesus Christ invade their sex life. And when they sense something's wrong in that aspect of their marriage, they spend all their time looking for a new technique because they have neglected their relationship. They've never let Jesus Christ deliver them from themselves so they're free to flow into the life of their partner in the most intimate relationship on earth.

How does being a Christian relate to your thought life? Both at the seminary and as I travel I find young men and women who've filled their minds with garbage, and then they ask me, "How come I'm not holy?" Not long ago I said to a young man who has consistently read *Playboy* and *Penthouse*, "Do you really think that's going to make you a man of God?"

How about your diet? If I scheduled a seminar at your church and then walked in drunk, you'd dismiss me immediately. But if I walked in fifty pounds overweight, you'd feed me more, right? Sure—after all, you can't have a Christian gathering without food. Did you ever wonder how the early church made it without coffee and doughnuts? I'll tell you: They had something better to provide togetherness—persecution. That'll weld you together in a hurry. But maybe this is too convicting. On to something else.

How about exercise? Dr. Kenneth Cooper, who popularized the aerobics concept, has a solid Christian testimony. He told an audience of about three to four hundred students at our seminary that by a regular, systematic exercise program they could each add five to fifteen years to their ministry. Think of the implications!

You also need rest—and not just sleep, but a change of pace. I came across a simple but interesting grid that has helped me seek a balance in my life:

How much of my time do I spend with people?	How much of my time do I spend alone?
How much of my time do I spend at work?	How much of my time do I spend at play?

Most of us tend to be off balance in at least one of these areas.

I once visited one of my former students to join him for a week of ministry meetings. As soon as I arrived, his wife got me aside and said, "Will you please say something to my husband? He's averaging only five hours of sleep a night and is headed for four, and…frankly, we can't live with him. He's driving the kids up a wall."

Near the end of the week he and I were traveling in the car together, and as he drove, I said to him, "Hey, man, how come you don't smoke?"

We almost went off the highway. "Prof," he finally answered, "I never smoke."

"Yes," I said, "I noticed I hadn't seen you light up a single time all week."

By then he was giving me some rather strange looks, as if he thought I had squirrels crawling around in my steeple.

"Why don't you smoke?" I asked.

"Prof," he said, "my body is the temple of the Holy Spirit."

"Yeah," I said, "that's right. Fantastic. Good thinking." Then I added, "Is that also the reason you're averaging five hours of sleep a night, headed for four, and driving your family bonkers?"

I wouldn't have jarred him as much if I had dropped a two-by-four on his head.

Your Social Dimension

How about the social dimension of your life? Who do you have in terms of friends?

Do you fellowship only with Baptists? ("After all, they're God's chosen people; the others are God's frozen people.")

Got any friends among the unsaved?

Our studies on effective relational evangelism show that the average person coming to Christ is good for only two years. After that, he's dropped all of his lost friends. Or they have dropped him. Usually the former.

Do you know any lost people? You say, "Well, I'm a preacher." But that doesn't excuse you from being a Christian. Try being something other than what your position is, and don't let it get in the way. Try being a person for a while.

I don't know if your experience matches ours, but Jeanne and I have found that socially speaking, one of the most difficult things to get involved in constructively is a Christian group. Some of our groups are so inane that we insult each other's intelligence.

So I encourage you to do some creative thinking in regard to your friendships and acquaintances and see what God will do with it.

How about friends in different age groups? Do you know any little kids? I mean, really *know* them, so they call you Uncle Dan or whomever, and they think you're the greatest?

Know any teenagers? Most of us are scared to death of teenagers. When Jeanne and I had four of them at one time and invited guests over, I'd tell them beforehand, "Look, you need to understand that when you come, you're gonna have four pairs of teenage eyes staring down your throat. If that's threatening to you, you may want to bail out now."

"No, no, that's all right.... Do they bite?"

"I don't know. Come on over. We'll find out."

So enrich your circle of friends. And while we're on the subject, let me give you a true test of a close friend. A close friend is someone who

...knows everything about you, yet totally accepts you;

...will listen to your most heretical ideas without rejecting you;

...and knows how to criticize you in a way you'll listen.

It took me ten years before I let Jeanne become my best friend because I was scared to death to let her know what I was really like and what were my deep fears and anxieties. "If she ever finds out," I thought, "she'll reject me."

Then it finally dawned on me: She already knew!...yet totally accepted me. That freed me up.

How Am I Doing?

Finally, remember that the unexamined life is not worth living.

In our home we had what I suspect you have in yours if you're a parent— a growth chart to mark the kids' heights. Ours was on the back side of a closet door. In fact, when we sold the house, we took the door down, replaced it with a new one, and took the marked-up door with us.

Once when Bev, our second daughter, was quite small but quite interested in growth, she promised me she would grow while I was gone on a ministry trip for a couple of weeks. When I returned and stepped off the plane, she greeted me with "Daddy, come home quick! We gotta see how much I growed!" So we went home to the closet door and measured. It couldn't have been more than a few millimeters, but she jumped up and down. "Daddy, I told you, I did grow!"

Then we went into the living room for a special time of talking, and she asked me one of those questions you wish kids wouldn't ask: "Daddy, why do big people stop growing?"

I don't know what I told her, but I'm sure it was very superficial: "Well, you need to understand, Bev, they stop growing up but not out—you know, a nice dresser, but their middle drawer is sticking out."

But long after she was gone, God was working me over with her words. Why *do* big people stop growing? What is it with me? Why do seminary professors stop growing? They often do, you know, just like anyone else. Why?

It's a danger for all teachers. I've had people say to me, "Brother Hendricks, I've been teaching in this department for twenty-three years." Well what does that necessarily prove? I'll tell you what: the grace of God, that's all. Long ago I learned that if you take zero and multiply it by any number, you've still got zero.

After all, experience does not necessarily make you better; in fact it tends to make you worse, unless it's *evaluated* experience.

The good teacher's greatest threat is satisfaction—the failure to keep asking, "How can I improve?" The greatest threat to your ministry is *your ministry*.

So don't be so busy doing things that you don't *become* someone significant. Don't hesitate to go back to the drawing board and ask, "Lord, how am I doing—in light of what *you* want me to be?"

As with all evaluation, any self-examination should be built on three questions: (1) What are my strengths? (2) What are my weaknesses? (3) What do I have to change?

And remember: The process of change is essentially the process of altering your habit patterns. If you do something once, you can do it twice. Do it twice, and you can do it three times. Do it three times, and you're beginning to make a habit of it.

Empty Pedestals

In a barber shop recently I struck up a conversation with a boy I'd seen there before. After a while I asked, "Who do you want to be like?"

"Mister," he said, "I ain't found nobody I want to be like."

And he's not an exception. If you're out there in the battle, you know what I'm talking about. Kids aren't looking for a perfect teacher, just an honest one, and a growing one. Yet for so many of them, the pedestals are empty.

Our land is covered over today with young people—and adults as well—who are broken at the wheel, who have no clue why Jesus Christ came to visit our planet, who don't know the Bible has answers for their problems.

Their screaming need is to see men and women who know the living word of God, who are constant students of that Book, and who allow it to grip them so they grow to hate what God hates and to love what God loves.

And as that truth—personally embraced—begins to transform them, they make an impact.

he true

function of the teacher is to

create the most favorable

conditions for self-learning....

True teaching is not that which

gives knowledge, but that

which stimulates pupils to gain

it. One might say that he

teaches best who teaches least.

JOHN MILTON GREGORY

2

The Law of Education

As an effective teacher, you must not only know that which you would teach—that is, your content—but you must also know those whom you wish to teach.

You are not interested simply in inculcating principles; you want to infect people.

Therefore, *the way people learn determines how you teach.* This is the Law of Education.

The concept behind this law is what John Milton Gregory in his classic work *The Seven Laws of Teaching* calls the Law of the Teaching Process. It involves stimulating and directing *the learner's self-activities*—that's the key expression.

In fact, we can further define the law this way: The teacher must excite and direct the learner's self-activities, and, as a rule (though I'll give some exceptions later), *tell the learner nothing—and do nothing for him—that he can learn or do for himself.* Therefore, what's important is not what you do as a teacher, but what the learners do as a result of what you do.

This definition casts both teacher and learner into well-defined roles:

The teacher is primarily a stimulator and motivator...not the player, but the coach who excites and directs the players.

The learner is primarily an investigator, a discoverer, and a doer.

So, again, the ultimate test of teaching is not what you do or how well you do it, but what and how well the learner does.

My oldest daughter, Barb, took violin lessons from the first-chair violinist in the Dallas Symphony Orchestra, and it cost me a bundle. When recital time came, who do you think performed? Not him. I never heard him play at a single recital I attended...never heard him say, "Ladies and gentlemen, let me show you how well I've mastered this violin." No—I wasn't paying him to *play*, but to teach Barb, and what I wanted to know was how well she could play as a result of what he taught her.

Good teachers can't be focused on what *they* do, but on what their students are doing.

Plato said something you ought to commit to memory: "What is honored in a country is cultivated there." So what do you honor in those you teach? Do you settle for the fact that they can give you all the right answers and mouth all the Christian truths? Does that satisfy you?

It bothers some of my students at the seminary that I'm never impressed with how much they know. They're always throwing in Greek and Hebrew here and there to impress me, and I say, "Big deal. How does it work in your life?"

But that's not often the emphasis in our educational system today in which teaching is telling and testing is essentially a cramming meter—teachers are interested in how much a student can cram into his head and then regurgitate onto a piece of paper. In a hallway at the seminary I once met a student on his way to an exam. He seemed to be in a trance, and I started to put my arm around him and talk to him. "Prof," he joked, "don't touch me! I'll leak everything I know."

That's not education.

Many people who have never sat inside a college classroom are brilliantly educated. They are men and women of wisdom, and they have received—and are receiving—an education. They may not know everything, but what they know, they live—and God is using them as his instruments to accomplish his purposes.

The Tension

Psychologist Abraham Maslow pointed out four levels of learning.

The learner's beginning point, the basic level where everyone starts, is *unconscious incompetence*—that is, you're ignorant and you don't know it.

The next level is *conscious incompetence*—now you know you don't know.

How do you find out? Usually somebody tells you, but occasionally you discover it for yourself.

The third level is *conscious competence*—you have learned something, as when you first got the hang of driving a car, and you're consciously aware of it as you do it.

The final level is *unconscious competence*—you're so competent you don't even think about it anymore: You get in your car, turn the ignition key, release the brake, operate the gear shift, and go through a whole series of coordinated activities without ever thinking about them. In fact, most of your time driving is spent thinking about something other than driving.

The art of teaching—and the difficulty of learning—is getting people to place themselves at the beginning of that cycle, to plunge to the bottom, so they can start the learning process.

It won't be easy—for you or for them. But there is no growth, there is no development, there is no learning...without *tension*. Tension is absolutely indispensable to the process.

To be sure, too much tension leads to frustration, stress, anxiety. But too little tension produces apathy.

So God moves into our lives by divine design, to periodically disturb our equilibrium. That's how he develops us.

We pray, "Lord, make me like your Son," then get up from our prayer and go out, and everything in life comes unglued. "Lord," we say, "what happened?" What happened is that he's answering our prayer. Remember that Jesus Christ, although he was a son, learned obedience by the things he suffered.

Do you keep the people in your class feeling comfortable? Or do you let their equilibrium be disturbed so they realize *I've got to study God's word more and think more; I've got to try this out in real life?*

One of the things I use extensively as a teacher is role-playing. Jeanne and I were team teaching a class for about five hundred seminary wives. We took turns speaking, each one of us teaching a short section followed by the other doing the next one. At one point when Jeanne began speaking I looked at her and said sternly, "Jeanne, we agreed not to do this part."

"Howie," she said sharply, "this is exactly what we decided on before we got up here." We began to argue.

A silent air of tension immediately gripped that audience. The room was full of it. If a match had been lit, we would have been the next humans on the moon.

When we finally broke it—and they realized the argument was planned—the place exploded in applause. We had not been afraid to expose ourselves; we dared to admit we knew something about how to argue with each other. And the resulting tension had heightened the learning.

Incidentally, a role-playing situation can really open up learner involvement. One of my students tried it when he was teaching a class on marriage communication at a Baptist church. He invited a couple from the seminary, a couple no one else in the class knew, to come in as visitors. While he was lecturing, the couple began whispering hotly to one another.

"What did you bring me here for?" the man said.

"Keep quiet!" she responded.

"I told you I didn't want to hear any of this religious jazz," he shot back.

Suddenly another man in the class leaned over and said to the husband, "Give her h___, man!"—which was not exactly a part of the program.

What in the World Are You Trying to Do?

I once went to preach in a church on the West Coast, and as I got up to speak, I found this sign facing me on the lectern: "What in the world are you trying to do to these people?" It nearly derailed my message.

Afterward I asked the church's pastor about the sign. He said, "Hendricks, I've been preaching for twelve years without an objective, and it finally dawned on me one day that if I didn't know what I was doing, there was a good possibility they didn't know what *they* were supposed to do. So I've started coming into the pulpit with clear-cut objectives."

How about you? Do you have clear-cut objectives for your teaching? Do you know how to give a true education?

I'll suggest for you three basic goals, and though I don't want you to buy them on the spot, I dare you to interact with them. If you think about them enough and they become your personal property as a teacher, then in succeeding generations there'll be people who rise up and call you blessed.

Goal number one: *Teach people how to think.*

If you want to change a person permanently, make sure his thinking changes, and not merely his behavior. If you change only his behavior, he won't understand why he's made the change. It's only superficial, and usually short-lived.

Your task as a teacher is to stretch the human mind—which, by the way, is like a rubber band; once you stretch it, it never quite returns to its original form.

I'm acquainted with many students who are afraid they're going to strain their brain...to wear that baby out through overuse. But I have news for them. I once asked a pathologist friend in Philadelphia, "Have you seen many brains?"

"Hundreds of them," he said.

"Have you ever seen one worn out?"

"I've never seen one even slightly used," he answered.

So go ahead and run the risk.

Now, when we speak of stretching the mind, we're not talking simply about rearranging prejudices. That's what most people perceive thinking to be. No, we're talking about an exacting process...a process of planting seeds that will germinate, and—interestingly enough—bear fruit. When? You never know. That's the excitement of teaching.

I've had former students come to me and say, "You changed the whole course of my life."

"Man, that's encouraging," I tell them. "What did I say to change the course of your life?" Then they repeat some profound statement, and I have to say, "I can't remember ever saying it, but that's tremendous! Let me write it down."

If you think about it, the people you recall as the best teachers in your life were probably those who planted seeds—and you're still reaping the harvest from them.

Don't ever get so hung up on a specific lesson that you forget this fact: *Good teaching—and true education—consists simply of a series of teachable moments.* There's a dynamic of unpredictable timing involved so that when you break through to the learner's mind and heart, a readiness to learn is there.

Mark 4 is the classic illustration—the parable of the sower. Reading that parable you discover there is only one variable in each situation Jesus describes. The sower is the same, and the seed is the same, but in each case the soil—the individual's response—is different. Everything hangs on the response of the individual.

Whatever you do, be prepared to exploit those teachable moments by helping responsive individuals learn to think. And please note: If you're going to teach them how to think, that presupposes you know how to think yourself.

I was changed permanently because of some of the professors I had in college and seminary, and in many cases it had nothing to do with the subject they taught. But it had everything to do with the fact that I was exposed to a human being who knew how to think and who had the incredible idea that he could teach me to do the same.

Christianity—and evangelical Christianity in particular—has been given a bad rap intellectually. Nothing could be further from the truth, but many people view Christianity as the nonthinking person's filter. They think becoming a Christian means you have to put your head in a bucket and fire a .45 into it. (This is particularly the view regarding women. In parts of the evangelical community today I think I would scream if I were a woman, knowing that if I went to church and asked, "What can I do for Jesus Christ," they would tell me to make cookies.)

But Jesus reminded us we are to love the Lord our God with all our heart, soul, strength, and mind. So no Christian can follow Christ and still throw his mind into neutral.

A second goal: *Teach people how to learn.* Create learners who will perpetuate the learning process for the rest of their lives.

Think for a moment what's involved in learning. Learning is always a process. It's going on all the time. Every moment you live, you learn; and as you learn, you live. Stop learning today, and you stop living tomorrow.

That's why I commend you for reading this book. It's the greatest compliment you could give me about yourself. So often the people in our churches who *most need to learn* are those who seldom try to. Isn't that interesting? But you have chosen otherwise. Congratulations! You're involved in the process, and it's a thrilling one. It will keep you alive.

Not only is it an exciting process, but it's also a logical one. Ideally, it follows three steps: It goes from the whole, to the part, and back to the whole. This is what we call *synthesis*. It moves from the big picture to an analysis of the parts—breaking them down, seeing their meaning in light of the whole—to putting them back together again so everyone walks out the door thinking, "Now I understand it and can use it."

So to get people involved in the process of learning, give them first the big picture. Some people—sharp, articulate, capable individuals—have been in our churches all their lives and still don't know the name of the game, because it's the breaking down into parts that we tend to specialize in.

Once when I was invited to speak at a church, the elders said, "Hendricks, would you do us a favor? Promise not to preach from Ephesians."

I decided to josh them a bit. "You know," I said, "I never go to a church where they tell what I can or cannot preach."

"Oh, no, no, you don't understand," they said. "You see, we've been in Ephesians for three years—and we're just beginning the second chapter."

That's par for the course…and it's why most people in our churches end up with nothing more than twelve baskets of fragments. They don't have the big picture.

Not only is the learning process exciting and logical, but it's also a discovery process. Truth is always most profitable and productive when you can see it for yourself.

For more than three decades I've taught a course at Dallas Seminary on "How to Study the Bible for Yourself." It's the most enjoyable course I've ever been privileged to teach. After studying an assigned passage on their own, the students come back to class, and there's never enough time to share all they've found.

I'll often have a student say, "Dr. Hendricks, I'll bet you haven't seen this before." (He's thinking John Calvin and Martin Luther never had a clue about it either.) And after he relates a gem of truth gleaned from the text, you've never seen a seminary professor get as enthusiastic as I do.

But what do some of us do with a person like that? We tell him, "Yes, Bill, that's good. In fact, fifty-three years ago, when I first met Jesus, I learned that truth too."

As a result, the average listener in evangelical churches is not excited by the truth—he's embalmed by it. The educational program in the churches is often an insult to people's intelligence. We're giving them wilted cut flowers instead of teaching them how to grow by means of God's word, which is alive! They've never had the experience of *discovery learning* in the word of God…of saying personally, "This is what God has said. This is what he wants me to do. Somebody's got to hear about it and experience the kind of changes in life that I'm experiencing!"

The third objective: *Teach people how to work.*

That brings us back to the principle of never doing anything for a student that he is capable of doing for himself. If you do, you'll make him or her an educational cripple…a pedagogical paraplegic.

If you've ever been to Yellowstone National Park, you were probably given a piece of paper by a ranger at the park entrance. On it in big letters was the warning "Do Not Feed the Bears." You no sooner drive into the heart of the park, however, than you see people feeding the bears. When I first saw this, I asked a ranger about it. "Sir," he answered, "you have only a small part of the picture." He described how the park-service personnel in the fall and winter have to carry away the bodies of dead bears, bears who have lost their ability to fend for food.

That's what's happening to us.

I want to ask you a question. It may be convicting, so fasten your seat belt.

Are you one of the culprits in this? Are you a part of the problem, or are you working on the solution?

Never forget that your task is to develop people who are self-directed, who are disciplined, who do what they do because they choose to do it. That's why I suggest you spend more time questioning answers than answering questions. Our job is not to give quick-and-easy answers, patent-medicine solutions that never work in the realities of life. It's far, far better to have students leave your class scratching their heads with questions they think and talk about, and with problems they're eager to find solutions for in the week ahead.

Then you know you've got some *education* going on—rather than the polite yawns you usually get.

And before we leave the subject—be assured that it takes work to get people to work.

Basic Skills

If you're going to teach students to think, to learn, and to work, then help them master four basic skills: reading, writing, listening, and speaking.

Evangelical churches today desperately need people who read. I want to make a prophecy: By the end of this century, more and more of our churches will be forced to teach remedial reading to their people.

One day I said to one of my classes in seminary, "The problem with the average guy coming out of the university is that he can't read, he can't write, and he can't think. And if you can't read, write, or think, what can you do?"

"Watch television," someone answered.

That's exactly right. And television is eating our lunch educationally. As a Christian educator, and especially if you're a parent, you should be stabbed awake by the reality that our people are addicted to a plug-in drug, and one of the best things you can do is help get them off it. That sad set can decimate not only their ability to read, but also their ability to think and to create—the most essential skills you as a teacher want to develop in them.

Of course there's a lot in common educational practice that fails to develop those abilities as well. My oldest son, Bob, was so eager when it was time for him to begin the first grade. "Daddy," he said, "I'm going to learn how to read!"

He came home the first day and said dejectedly, "Daddy, I can't read."

"You know, Son," I reassured him, "it's going to take a little while. Hang in there, Buddy."

But as the months went by and he still wasn't reading, I became concerned. I went down to talk to the teacher, a lovely young lady, freshly minted from a school of education.

"Oh, Mr. Hendricks," she said, "you don't understand. The important thing is not that he learn how to read, but that he be happy." "Oh no," I thought, "we're up against the happiness cult." We put up with it till the end of the year, when I finally asked the teacher, "Did it ever occur to you, Madam, that he would be happier if he knew how to read?" This apparently had never dawned on her.

I spent six hundred dollars for a course in remedial reading for him—the best six hundred I ever invested because today he can read faster than I do (which is very fast), and when we're together we have extremely stimulating discussions about what we're reading.

Growing out of the skill of reading is that of writing. Give your students creative opportunities to express themselves on paper. You'll be fascinated by what some of them can produce.

Of the other two skills—listening and speaking—listening is the more difficult, the greater art, and the more crucial skill. Yet we seldom teach people how to listen, and furthermore we don't model it for them.

The average business executive spends 70 percent of his time listening, for which he gets little or no training. Go to almost any college, and you can't get out of the place without taking a speech course. But almost none of them compels you to take a course in listening.

I've taught speech for years, and I tell you it is relatively simple to teach a person to speak. But try teaching him to listen!

In seminary we teach homiletics—the science of the preparation and delivery of sermons—and the result is preaching. Now preaching, of course, is thoroughly biblical. We can't get out of doing it. It's not an option. But what good is preaching if nobody listens?

Furthermore, a good teacher is a good listener. Not many people will tell you that, so take it by faith.

As for speaking, this is an area of training which, ideally, parents should begin early in the home. I suggest they begin getting their children on their feet and talking when they're just three or four or five. Later on, take them out to hospitals or to the local jail or other places where they have opportunities to articulate their faith. You learn to speak by speaking.

A Foundation Called Failure

Failure is a necessary part of the learning process.

I have four children. Do you know how they learned to walk? One day when they were in a playpen behind bars, they watched intensely as someone walked across the room. They said to themselves, "My, look at that amazing peripatetic action!" So each one got up and said, "I shall now proceed to walk." And they've been doing it ever since.

You don't believe that, of course. You've watched a little kid pull himself up, let go, and waddle a few steps, then down he goes. He gets up again, and across the room you extend your arms and say, "Come on, Billy!" He starts coming, but soon his legs are going faster than his bod, and he sprawls on the floor.

Does he then say, "Shucks! I guess I was never called to walk"? No, he gets up and walks, and he falls, and he walks, and the more he learns to walk the less he falls—though the time never comes when falling is not a live option.

Picture the situation: The disciples have been sent out two by two, and they're having a ball. They come back to Jesus and say, "Lord, even the demons are subject to us!"

But one day they run into a difficult case. They're unable to cast out a demon from a boy. The boy's father in exasperation goes to Jesus and says, "I went to your disciples, but they were not able." So Jesus casts the demon out.

Sure enough, the disciples get Jesus off to the side and say, "Lord, what happened?"

"I'll tell you," he says. "This kind comes out by prayer and fasting only." As so often happened, the disciples' taste of failure provided one of their greatest learning experiences.

One of the most brilliant students I ever taught is now a professor at a leading university, and is fast becoming the world's foremost authority in his field. He took a course from me which he failed royally. And to this day he will tell you it was the greatest learning experience of his life.

Special Cases

Teaching is both a science and an art. As a science, it involves basic laws. As an art, it involves knowing the exceptions to the laws.

There are exceptions to the principle of never telling students—or doing for them—what they can learn or do for themselves, and if you know the exceptions, you'll avoid some frustration.

One exception involves simply the matter of saving time. There's no need to waste hours reinventing the wheel. And if the building we're in catches fire, that is not the time for a brainstorming session on what to do. It's time for someone to say, "Here's the exit!" The same is true in good teaching.

A second exception concerns students with special needs for encouragement and help. For various reasons, as these students get involved in the challenging process of learning—which of necessity involves experiencing failure—they are more likely to give up. In the process of failing it's easy for them to say, "I know I can't make it."

I was once asked in a television interview what I had learned in thirty-five years of teaching at a seminary. I said I had learned that my primary task is to convincingly tell the student, "I believe in you! You're going to make it!" Seminary students—men and women who represent what could be considered the cream of the crop in the evangelical community—are today often shot through with inferiority feelings.

So, in your teaching, be sensitive to the man or woman who says, "I don't think God can use me," or the kid who says, "I'd like to be a lawyer or a missionary, but I don't think I have what it takes." It's so easy to destroy that person's spirit.

A third exception is when your students are so highly motivated they'll take in everything you feed them and still want more. They are so turned on, and their interest is so intense, they can hardly contain themselves.

I once gave a New Testament to a former professional football player who had come to Christ and whose life changed radically. A week after I gave it to him, we met again and he said to me, "I read it."

"Great," I said, "now you'll want to keep reading in it until you've read it all."

"No," he said, "I read the whole thing—including the Psalms at the back." He continued, "I understand there's another half." So I got him a complete Bible, and four weeks later he had read through the entire Old Testament as well. (I know of elders in evangelical churches who've never read through the Bible once in their entire lives!)

So when the student is that hungry, tell him or her all you can.

No Turning Back

Finally, a word of warning: Though it may take time, once you get people over the barrier and into the true joy of discovery and learning, they can never again settle for education that's less exciting. They'll never be satisfied with anything less than a deep involvement in the learning process.

nowledge

cannot be passed like a

material substance from one

mind to another, for thoughts

are not objects which may be

held and handled....

Ideas must be rethought,

experience must be

re-experienced.

JOHN MILTON GREGORY

3

The Law of Activity

Your task as a communicator is not to impress people, but to *impact* them; not just to convince them, but to *change* them.

Christian education today is entirely too passive. And that's incongruous, because Christianity is the most revolutionary force on the planet. It *changes* people.

Yet frequently we've taken this most revolutionary force on earth and set it in concrete. The average Christian's attitude is well expressed when he sings, "As it was in the beginning, is now and ever shall be." Churches and Christianity often resist the very changes they are meant to bring about.

Romans 8 informs me that every believer is predestined to become conformed to the image of Jesus Christ. If that's really true, then how much change should we rightfully expect?

Maximum Involvement → *Maximum Learning*

If teaching were only telling, my children would be incredibly brilliant; I've told them everything they need to know. That's probably true with most parents. I can hear the father yelling, "How many times have I told you that, Son?" And his teenager replies casually, "Don't know, Dad. Computer broke down."

But the teaching-learning process is something more.

The Law of Activity tells us that *Maximum learning is always the result of maximum involvement.* That's true, with one condition: The activity in which the learner is involved must be meaningful.

This condition implies an important insight about teaching: Activity in learning is never an end in itself; it's always a means to an end.

"We've really got the students busy!" the teacher says proudly.

"Doing what?" asks the observer.

"Nothing, but they're sure having a ball!"

Never forget your *purpose*. Your objective determines your outcome. You achieve that for which you aim.

For some years I was a board member of an aimless organization that had existed for a quarter of a century. Eventually I began thinking, "What in the world is the purpose of this thing?"

Finally at one board meeting I said, "Men, what's the purpose of this organization?"

"Well, Brother Hendricks, that's a good question. Brother Brown, you've been here longer than any of the rest of us. What would you say is the purpose of this organization?" We went around the table trying to answer that question, and no one could give a clear and compelling answer. So I said, "May I make a motion?"

"Oh yes, a motion is always in order."

"I move we bury this thing."

"But Brother Hendricks, we've been going for twenty-five years!"

"Then that's twenty-five of the finest reasons I can think of for burying it." I got off the board, but they're still going—for what purpose, I'll never know.

Purposeful activity implies quality activity. Think for a moment about these three statements, and ask yourself how, if possible, you could improve each one:

    1. *Practice makes perfect.*

    2. *Experience is the best teacher.*

    3. *We learn by doing.*

As for Statement 1—no, practice doesn't really make perfect; what it makes is *permanent*. If you play tennis or golf, you can practice for years and never improve your game *if you're practicing the wrong way*. You need a coach to point out how to better place your feet or turn your wrist or hold your racquet. Then you'll improve. So a truer statement would be, *Well-guided practice makes perfect.*

Regarding Statement 2, experience is certainly a good teacher. But you don't have to get hooked on cocaine to be aware of its devastation, and even many who are hooked don't understand the danger. So a better way to say it is, *Properly evaluated experience is the best teacher.*

As far as I can trace it, Plato was the first person in recorded history to give us Statement 3. And yes, we do learn by doing, but we may learn the wrong things. Therefore, a better statement is, *We learn by doing the right things.* To be sure, we sometimes learn by doing the wrong things, but that learning can easily be destructive rather than constructive.

So there is a direct correlation between learning and doing. The higher the learner's involvement, the greater his potential for learning. The best learners are participators; they're not merely watching the action from the outside, but are deeply engrossed in it, involved to the hilt. They're also enjoying it more than learners who aren't involved.

Suppose I wanted you to learn more about the Holy Land, and I gave you three choices as to the method.

First, a lecture on the Holy Land. Now don't reject that option offhand. I'm an authority in this area and have studied it for years. I have historical and archaeological data that I think would impress you.

Option two is a photographic slide presentation. I have photos that are real grabbers, plus good music to go with it. And the show even ends with a Mediterranean sunset.

The third option: You accompany me personally on a trip to the Holy Land, and see it for yourself. I believe I know which one you would choose.

I Do—And I Change

This Law of Activity is confirmed by a great deal of modern research in educational psychology, as well as by an ancient Chinese proverb:

I hear, and I forget.

I see, and I remember.

I do, and I understand.

I would make one addition to that proverb. In my judgment, when you *do*, the result is more than understanding; you also *change*.

Psychologists tell us we have the potential of remembering only up to 10 percent of what we hear. And that's *potential*, not actual. As a matter of fact, if you do remember 10 percent of what you hear, you're in the genius category.

Unfortunately, the bulk of Christian education is hearing oriented. That's why it's often so inefficient.

If we add seeing to hearing, psychologists say our potential for remembering goes up to 50 percent. That's why visual aids are so important. We live in a visually oriented society. The average person I teach in seminary has spent more time watching television than he has spent in classrooms from kindergarten through college. That's a massive dose of TV—and it can be lethal because it's so subtle, so pervasive. And because of the true effectiveness of seeing combined with hearing, those who repeatedly watch television can gradually become brainwashed by what they see.

What about adding *doing* to seeing and hearing? The psychologists say this combination brings the percentage of memory up to 90 percent—and decades of teaching in a graduate institution have given me all the evidence I need to be convinced that's exactly true.

In over thirty years I have never given an examination in the seminary course on "How to Study the Bible for Yourself." That blows the minds of other professors. How in the world can you possibly teach without giving an exam? Very simple: Just get the students actively involved in the learning process.

I learned early on that students can memorize materials in any way you ask them to, and on an exam they can tell you it all. You can give them a great big A for it. Brilliant. Yet give them the same examination three days later, and they couldn't pass it if their lives depended on it.

But after getting students involved in the process, I've tested them twenty-five years later, and they still know and are using the same Bible study principles they learned in my class—and which they never memorized. They learned by usage. They learned in the process of activity.

The same is true in other aspects of the Christian life. The finest way to learn to witness, for example, is by witnessing, not by reading books about witnessing.

Have you ever read one of those books on evangelism? They're always loaded with illustrations. A guy gets on a plane, sits down in his seat, and fifteen minutes later the man sitting next to him comes to Christ. A half-hour more and the entire row is born again. An hour goes by, and all the flight attendants have received Christ. By the time they land, the whole planeload is saved.

The average person reads this and thinks, "You know, I'd better try that." So he does—trying to go exactly by the book—and it goes over like a lead balloon. He crawls back into his hole and says, "I guess I don't have the gift of evangelism."

No, to learn to witness, simply do it. Get involved in the process. That's the best way to learn anything.

Truth and life are always wedded in the Scripture. I love the way Paul spoke of it in Titus 1:1—"the truth that leads to godliness."

Jesus said, "He who has ears to hear, let him hear." The first time I read that I thought, "Lord, you've got to be kidding. What else do you do with ears? Collect wax? Hang earrings?" But Jesus had in mind something more.

When you read the word *hear* in the New Testament, you can also read it *do*. Because the Lord Jesus welded those words together when he said, "He that heareth my words and doeth them, he it is who loves me.... Why do you call me 'Lord, Lord,' and not do the things I tell you?" His implication? "Either stop calling me 'Lord,' or start doing what I ask you."

The name of the game in Christian education is not knowledge—it's active obedience.

I have a constant debate with the Lord. You see, I'm always trying to impress him with how much I know of his word, but for some strange reason he's never impressed.

Why should he be? Everything I know is the product of what he has revealed to me. And he's constantly reminding me of how little like Jesus Christ I am.

In the spiritual realm, the opposite of ignorance is not knowledge, it's obedience. In New Testament understanding, to know and not to do is not to know at all.

So the Lord says, "Hendricks, do you understand this?"

"Yes, Lord, I do."

"Good," he says. "The next move is yours."

Meaningful Activity

Let's look again at the Law of Activity: *Maximum learning is always the result of maximum involvement.* We said this law is true with one condition: The activity must be meaningful. What kinds of activities are meaningful?

I want to give five answers to that question—five forms of meaningful activity. Every one of them is available to you, no matter what kind of group you're teaching, or what subject.

1. *Activity that provides direction without dictatorship.*

When you give assignments—and you should—to get your students more involved in the learning process, remember to always provide a sphere of freedom. You want structure—not a straitjacket.

I'll often ask a student to study a certain passage of Scripture and to find and list principles from it. Then comes the response, "Dr. Hendricks, how many do you want?"

"I don't know," I say. "How many do *you* want?"

"Uhhh," he'll stammer, "but you're the professor."

"And *you're* the student. You're paying for this education, not me." It just blows all his circuits.

It generally takes me two to three years to turn a student like this around because he comes out of an educational system where the name of the game is to figure out what the teacher wants. It never occurs to him he's selling his educational soul down the river. Our students are working for the wrong people—for their teachers instead of for themselves.

So the ultimate question to the learner is "What do *you* want?" not "What does the teacher want?" Education must come from the individual learner. You as the teacher cannot pour it in. You have to *draw it out*. And by the way, "to draw out" is the root meaning of the word *education*.

I've taught a course in camping for seminary students, a fun course that offers some exciting times. We begin by looking at camping theory in the classroom and later take a canoe trip on the Brazos River.

"Now remember, men," I tell them in class, "one basic principle in canoeing is that of lashing in the stuff—lashing down all your gear inside the canoe so if the canoe turns over, your gear won't fall out. Got that?"

"Right, Prof. Here it is, right here in the notes."

"I'm glad you've got it in the notes. That's great. But what I want to know is, are you going to lash in the stuff? You know what it's like to sleep in a soggy bedroll?"

"Right, Prof, we've got it."

So out we go to the Brazos River and launch ten canoes. Would you believe…we're not on the river more than three minutes before four canoes flip over, three of which didn't have the stuff lashed in.

Following a not-so-wonderful evening of rest for those with wet sleeping bags, we all get up the next morning for breakfast. Now back in the classroom we had divided into groups, and I asked each one to plan their own menus for the trip—"whatever you think is best. It really doesn't make any difference, since most of what you cook will get burned anyway! But whatever you decide to cook, make sure you think through all the details concerning what you'll need."

So the guys who haven't slept all night are now ready to produce their long-planned pancake breakfast. But they've forgotten to bring the pancake turner. Plus, their fire isn't hot enough, so they've got gooey pancakes.

Have you ever watched someone using twigs to try to flip gooey pancakes? Most of them land in the fire. The rest are eventually thrown there.

I guarantee you, none of those guys will ever go camping again without taking a pancake turner.

So provide direction, not dictatorship. Let them hang themselves, if that's what it comes to. Great is the learning thereof.

2. *Activity that stresses function and application.*

That is, activity that immediately lets the learner put to use everything that's just been taught. Which implies that it's best not to teach at one time more than can be absorbed and used.

We're forever employing what I call Storage Tank Education. We think, "They've got to get all this information from ME, and they've got to get it all NOW." So we pour it on.

It's also called the Hamburger & Fan Treatment. All your ground beef goes on the blades, you turn on the fan…and the group gets sprayed.

Just like Jesus did it, right? Remember the occasion when he said to his disciples, "Look men, I'm only going to be with you three years. So get this stuff down now." No, of course you don't remember, because Jesus—the Personification of Truth—never did that. In fact he told them, "I've got many more things I'd like to share with you, but you're not able to bear them now. But that's no problem because when the Spirit of Truth comes, he'll guide you into all truth."

3. *Activity with a planned purpose.*

As we said before, objectives determine outcomes. You achieve that for which you aim.

Please note: Forget "busywork." Don't involve learners in activities for which there's no meaningful objective. There's nothing a human being resents more than busywork. And that's why, frankly, most Sunday school quarterlies could be used more profitably as kindling in your fireplace.

If you're teaching a class in which "requirements" are involved, ask yourself, "What's my objective?" What's to be accomplished by reading those books or doing that research or writing those reports? Do more words written and more books read make an education better? Or do we have those requirements simply because we've always had them? Many things done in the name of *scholarship* are meaningless.

In the same league with busywork is mere entertainment. As one student wrote on a research paper, "When is the church going to get out of the entertainment business? I don't go to church for entertainment. I can go to a good show in downtown Dallas if I want that."

I've been profoundly impressed with a program for high schoolers in a nearby church. It's one of the few I've seen that consistently throws down a challenge to the kids. They're never merely entertained. They're never babied. The group makes a tough training trip to Mexico every year. Everyone going has to learn Spanish, and a host of other requirements stretch the kids to the breaking point. But the kids love it. They take a bus with room for only twenty-five, yet eighty-seven kids signed up to go this past year.

4. *Activity that is concerned with the process as well as the product.*

Then students not only know WHAT they believe, but WHY.

If you give your students only the product—which is what we tend to specialize in—you limit them by your own limitations. But give them the process, and you launch them on a path with no limitations. They can, in fact, exceed you and become more effective than you.

One reason I've stayed so long in seminary teaching is the fulfillment of seeing so many of my students graduate and do far beyond what I could ever do. To build into their lives, and then to see them take that and run with it so much farther than I ever could, is true fulfillment.

A number of Christian youth organizations have sponsored research with results indicating a surprising similarity between Christian and non-Christian kids in the areas of values, morals, and behavior. The only major difference is a verbal one. The Christians answer no when asked if they would lie or cheat or steal or go to bed with someone, while the non-Christian kids say, "Of course, if it's to my advantage." But at the actual behavioral level, there is essentially no difference.

That's convicting, to say the least. Think through the implications. We're settling for the wrong things. We're settling for words. The Christian kids know all the shibboleths to get across Jordan, but they're missing out on the experience.

5. *Realistic activity that includes problem-solving situations.*

A student is seeking answers to whose questions? Yours? No, his. If we bring our own problems into the classroom for students to solve, they have no ownership of the solutions, and we're in danger of producing fake Christianity.

We often fail to get down to the real problems people have. So find out, *Where are they? What are they struggling with? What temptations are they facing?*

An increasing number of people in our churches right now are going down the moral tubes like hot grease. But how much are we talking about it—and teaching about it?

How many times do we teach about Bible characters as if they're fugitives from a wax museum? They're a collection of cardboard Christians who really don't have the problems and feelings we have.

So make the activities lifelike, and find the open sesame to people's hearts. But don't stack the case. Many times I've heard a teacher say, "Now boys and girls, what do you want? Do you want the will of God for your life, with peace and satisfaction and fulfillment and success? Or would you prefer your own will, with misery and poverty and emptiness?" Too many of us have never come to grips with how much fun sin can be.

Going On

You'll remember we said learning is a *process.* Don't drop one experience on people and then say, "Well, you got it. Wrapped that one up. Now what else can I teach you?"

The gospels tell us of the time Jesus and his disciples fed the five thousand. You know the story: They started with five loaves and two fish, and from that Jesus was able to satisfy five thousand hungry men, besides women and children. When everyone was thoroughly satisfied, they picked up twelve baskets of fragments—ending up with more food than they began with. An amazing miracle.

But a little further on we read, "The disciples had not understood about the loaves."

Then comes the feeding of the four thousand. Same story, though this time they start with seven loaves and a few small fish. But everyone is satisfied, and left over are seven baskets of fragments.

A little later it was obvious the twelve still had not learned what Jesus wanted them to learn from these miracles. "Don't you remember?" Jesus said. "When I broke the five loaves for the five thousand, how many basketfuls of fragments did you pick up?"

And they said, "Twelve."

"And when I broke the seven loaves for the four thousand, how many basketfuls that time?"

"Seven," they answered.

And Jesus said to them, *"How is it that you do not understand?"*

Recall as well the walking-on-water incident. Here are professional fishermen out on the water, and they look out and see what appears to be a ghost. They're scared to death. But Jesus tells them, "It is I."

Peter, in typical fashion, says, "Lord, if it's you, bid me come." Jesus says, "Come."

Letting go of that boat's gunnels was probably one of the hardest things Peter ever did. But he did it, and Philip and Andrew were probably back in the boat saying, "Man, look at Peter go!"

But then Phil yells out, "Watch out for that wave, Peter!" Peter sees it, freezes, and drops down a manhole. He then says the most beautifully concise prayer in the Bible: "Lord, save me." You can't eliminate a single word from it without changing the meaning. Can you imagine what would have happened if he had prayed one of those prayer-meeting prayers you often hear, where the guy is catching up on his prayer life, and he scrapes the Milky Way and takes a tour of the mission field and reviews his theology? Peter would have been twenty feet under by the time it was over.

Now let me ask you: How do you think Peter got back in the boat? Do you think Jesus carried him? No, he walked back, but I'll guarantee you he never took his eyes off the Savior.

That is learning.

I've often seen someone fall into something just like that hole in the water, and then I've seen that person emerge to become a man or woman who *believed* God. They realized they couldn't pull it off themselves. The Lord proved it to them through that failure in their expertise.

Studying the life of the Savior, the greatest Teacher, makes it clear that he didn't cram a lot of heads full of a collection of theological facts. No, he involved his disciples in the process so that later the pagan world was compelled to testify, "These are they who have turned the world upside down."

That's the challenge to Christian education as this century draws to a close.

t is the teacher's

mission... by sympathy, by example,

and by every means of influence

—by objects for the senses, by facts

for the intelligence—to excite the

mind of the pupils, to stimulate their

thoughts.... The greatest of teachers

said: "The seed is the word."

The true teacher stirs the ground

and sows the seed.

JOHN MILTON GREGORY

The Law of Communication

Malcolm Muggeridge noted a surprising feature held in common by almost all books on communication—"a singular incapacity to communicate."

Not long ago I read a tome—850 pages—on the communication process, which I recommend if you're having problems with insomnia. It's absolutely paralyzing.

But then, communication is no piece of cake. And if you have a healthy respect for the difficulty of this process, you'll pray more intelligently, you'll study and work harder, and you'll learn to trust God at a deeper level.

A company in Chicago went bankrupt only a year after making a two-million-dollar profit. The reason: They failed to understand what business they were in. They thought they were in the bobby-pin business instead of the hair-care business. When women stopped using bobby pins, the company was finished.

So don't forget what business we're in—the business of communication. Communication is the reason for our existence as teachers.

It's also our number one teaching problem.

Building Bridges

The word *communication* comes from the Latin word *communis*, meaning "common." Before we can communicate, we must establish commonness, commonality. And the greater the commonality, the greater the potential for communication.

Take Mike's example: Mike and his wife Beth are happily married and have four children, two boys and two girls. Mike also teaches an adult Sunday school class.

In that class are many people like Mary. She's divorced, a single parent of two sons. Mike's primary task as a teacher is to flow into the life of Mary and those like her. But he can't assume Mary is coming from the same place in life as he and Beth.

So Mike and Beth have to spend time with Mary to develop commonality, to find out what she's struggling with. They invite Mary and her two boys to come over for a backyard barbecue, and they talk. Later they ask Mary to go with them to a symphony concert. Then comes a fishing trip when Mary's two sons join Mike and his boys.

In the process, Mike and Beth develop a base of commonality with Mary. That's why Mike earns the right to communicate with Mary on Sunday mornings. He wins a hearing.

The classic biblical illustration is in John 4—Jesus and the woman of Samaria. Notice what they have in common: Both are thirsty.

"Would you give me a drink?" he asks. She's startled out of her skin. "How is it that you, a Jewish man, would ask me, a Samaritan woman, for a drink?"

Jesus takes all the initiative and assumes nothing. He proceeds to break down all the barriers—racial, religious, sexual, social, and moral—to establish a base for communication.

And that's your task as well. That's what we're all about.

It's a process of bridge building.

The Law of Communication compels that very process: *To truly impart information requires the building of bridges.*

Years ago I took my aunt to an evangelistic meeting—the first time I had ever gotten her to hear the gospel preached. At the end of his message, the evangelist said, "I want everyone to stand up," and everyone stood. Then he said, "Now I want all the Christians to sit down."

I watched my aunt's face as her eyes immediately turned to steel and her jaw stiffened in anger and embarrassment.

It took me three years to get her to listen to the preaching of the gospel again, and she came that time only because I was preaching it—"I know you'd never pull a trick like that on me," she said.

My friend, we've got to do our homework on how people out there feel. They're scared to death to come into our churches, and all my sympathy is with them.

Thought—Feeling—Action

I'd like to take this complicated communication process and put it in a more understandable form. But please understand that you're going to have to study this to master it, to make it your own property. One time through won't do it.

All communication has three essential components: intellect, emotion, and volition—in other words, *thought*, *feeling*, and *action*. So whatever it is I want to communicate to another individual, it involves

> ...something I know,
>
> ...something I feel,
>
> ...and something I'm doing.

If I know something thoroughly, feel it deeply, and am doing it consistently, I have great potential for being an excellent communicator. In fact, the more thoroughly I know the concept...the more deeply I feel it...and the more consistently I practice it...the greater my potential as a communicator.

But all three components must be present.

It's as if I'm a salesman—except that I'm selling concepts, not commodities; ideas, not items. And in order to sell them, I've really got to know them, and I've got to be deeply convinced they're worthwhile, and I've got to be putting them to use personally. They've got to be working for *me*.

This is the beginning place for communication.

As Christians who believe in the authority and inspiration of Scripture, we have a body of truth given by revelation, truth that is to be communicated with the world. So we don't have to manufacture the message. We have only to declare it. This is our greatest asset, and yet it also tends to be a particular communication problem in the evangelical community.

Why? Because most of us settle for communicating the message with the intellectual component only. We rely too heavily on words alone. We're convinced that if we tell people the right thing, it will automatically solve their problems. We're too weak in communicating through the emotional and volitional aspects—the *feeling* and *action* components—because it threatens us out of our socks.

The moment I mention emotions, for example, you may get a little edgy. You think I'm talking about *emotionalism*, but that's emotions out of control, and you ought to fear that. Anything out of control is dangerous. But emotions under control is the name of the game: "God so *loved* the world that he gave..."

The most effective communication always includes an *emotional* ingredient—the *feeling* factor, the *excitement* element. If I claim to be committed to the eternal truth of the word of God, then it must be reflected in my values, in what I prize, in where I put my time and my money, in what I get excited about.

So what do *you* get excited about?

I had a neighbor who spent all his extra time polishing his boat. Every time I came by he'd say, "Hey, Howie, come on over and look at my boat!" One day he told me he had thirty-eight coats of wax on that thing. Here was where his heart was. Take away that toy, and you would take away his anesthetic to deaden the pain of an empty life.

What about you? What turns your crank? Does it come through in your teaching?

I don't mean to be cruel, but I'm compelled to be honest: If all those involved in Christian teaching had to become salesmen and saleswomen to make a living, most of them would starve to death. We're teaching the most exciting truth in all the world—eternal truth—and doing it as if it were cold mashed potatoes.

You listen to some guy talking about supposedly the most important thing in all the world, and it sounds like item twenty-one on a priority list of twenty. You're just sure he doesn't feel it in his gut. And you think, "If this is exciting to him, I'd hate to see him when he's bored."

But if you really believe and feel your message, it will show. You'll use good gestures, for example. All kinds of books on public speaking will give you material on meaningful movements, but no one in the world, even the best authority, can teach you anything better than the gestures you'll use naturally and comfortably *if you really feel what you're saying.* And if you don't feel it, adding gestures will only make it a contrived performance. All you'll be doing is putting on an act, and people will see right through it.

You'll also smile occasionally if you really feel your message. You'll know that life is too short not to enjoy it. Unfortunately, when some of us get home to heaven, God is going to say, "I'm sorry you didn't enjoy it more. I really never intended it to be that grim."

Wherever I go I can expect to run into a Christian with a severe case of the blahs. His face looks like the frontispiece to the Book of Lamentations. I'll say, "How are you, man?"

"Oh, pretty good," he says, "under the circumstances."

"And what in the world," I ask, "are you doing under there?"

Not only has the truth failed to excite us, but it too often has failed to change our behavior. In 2 Corinthians 5:17 we read that anyone in Christ is a *new creation,* and we understand that this begins a process of growth. So what difference does Jesus Christ make in my home, for example? Am I a better father and a better husband, or am I just as obnoxious as I was before? If Christianity doesn't work in my home, then it doesn't work, period.

How about business? A man tells me he's a Christian businessman, and he cheats. I ask him how he accounts for that in terms of Christian principles.

"Hendricks," he says, "you don't understand. We are in *Rome!* And the verse says, 'When in Rome, do as the Romans do.'"

"Say, I've got another verse for you," I tell him. "'When in Rome as a Christian, *don't* do as the Romans do.'"

"Where did you get that one?" he says, and he's still looking for it.

The fact bears repeating: What you *are* is far more important than what you say or do. God's method is always incarnational. He loves to take his truth and wrap it in a person. He takes a clean individual and drops him or her in the midst of a corrupt society, and that person—because of what he knows, feels, and does—convincingly demonstrates the power of God's grace.

When I first moved to Texas many years ago, I once quoted the saying, "You can lead a horse to water, but you can't make him drink." A tall West Texan answered back, "Son, you're wrong. You can feed him salt."

Let me ask you: Do people ever walk away from your teaching so thirsty they can hardly wait to drink in God's word for themselves?

So every time you teach, ask yourself, "What do I know—and what do I want these students to know? What do I feel—and what do I want them to feel? What do I do—and what do I want them to do?"

Case in point: teaching the Golden Rule. It isn't a matter of getting your students to decide mentally, "I shall now proceed to practice the Golden Rule. Now that I know it, I can automatically live it."

But what does the Golden Rule mean? What's really involved in "doing unto others as you would have them do unto you"? Help your class think it through together:

▼ What does it look like in the understanding of our age group, in our experience, in our culture?

▼ How do we *feel* about it? Are we comfortable with it? Is it radical?

▼ How do we react in a typical situation that calls for living out the Golden Rule? What's our usual response? Let's explore it on the feeling level so we understand why we live the way we live and what the alternatives are.

▼ And finally, let's do the fascinating work of finding specific ways we can apply this. Let's set a goal to put this into practice during the next week. And when we're together again, we'll share with each other what happened—the successes and the failures, how we blew it and why, and how it isn't easy but is worth doing.

The Way with Words

So I have something in my mind, I feel it deeply, it totally controls my actions—and I want to share it with you.

The next step: I take that concept-feeling-action and translate it into *words*.

Words are symbols; we take those symbols and arrange them systematically in a particular order—a syntax, a grammar—and thus we have language as a communication tool. But we can't get hung up there. The symbols—the words—are not what we're trying to get across. It's not a *word* message we communicate, but a *life* message. We're in the life business, not the word business. The pagan world is weary of our words but desperately hungry for reality, and they'll line up at our door if they sense we have it.

And yet, words have a place. I'm often asked by someone if it's more important to witness by his lips or by his life.

"Let me ask you a question," I tell him. "Do you ever fly in an airplane?"

"Why, yes."

"Well which is more important to you: the right wing or the left wing?"

If witness through our lives alone was enough, then everyone exposed to Jesus Christ during his time on earth should have been converted. He was the only person who ever lived a perfect life, yet even he shared his message verbally as well.

So communication is both verbal (primarily speaking and writing) and nonverbal (actions and "body language"), and both these forms must be congruent: What you say must correspond with what they see.

Jesus Christ never did anything that contradicted what he said. His actions and his words were always in perfect harmony.

As your teacher I may say, "You know, I'm really interested in you; in fact, I love you." But if I never prepare well for teaching your class and am never available to talk with you outside class, my verbal message that sounded so good is exterminated by my nonverbal message.

By the way, research has shown that our words account for only 7 percent of everything we communicate to others. This may be hard to take if you're like Old MacDonald's wife: talk-talk here, talk-talk there, everywhere talk-talk. (Here's a warning to many laymen and laywomen: You may be guilty of preaching without a license. Watch it, or the preachers' union will be after you.)

Teaching, therefore, involves a delicate balance and relationship between content and communication, between facts and form, between what you teach and how you teach it.

Is your method in keeping with the nature of your message? To be sure, you don't want to speak in a beautiful way but have nothing to say. On the other hand, how tragic it is to clothe the unsearchable riches of Jesus Christ with rags.

Perfecting Your Communication

Let's review the process: We take concepts and feelings and actions, translate them into words, then communicate them through speech—which requires two things: *preparation* and *presentation*.

1. *Preparation* is the best insurance you can take out on your communication. In preparation you give your message form and features. Your message needs structure; it needs to be packaged, and the ability to package your content is what separates the men from the boys and the women from the girls in communication.

You need an introduction—something that will capture them—bang! It could be a question, a quotation, a problem, something right out of their lives that will hook them. Don't just assume they'll be interested.

If I begin like this—"I'd like to tell you an illustration to sort of begin today. It's a very important illustration. In fact, it really meant a great deal to me. Just the other day I was reading in the Old Testament, and it just kind of leaped off the page and grabbed me, and so…"—what have I said so far? Nothing.

Here's a better beginning: "Elisha was residing in Dothan. He awakened early one morning, went out to pick up the *Dothan Daily*, and saw what to him was a horrible sight." Already you've driven to the heart of a story, and the class is right with you.

Now, this advice to have a good introduction presupposes that you know *what* you're going to say and *how* to say it for the rest of the time. In my judgment, almost every message I've heard could have been reduced in length by at least one-fourth, and in most cases more, if the speaker had known better *how* to say what he wanted to say.

You also need a conclusion—the least prepared part of most sermons and messages. How often I've heard a preacher say near the end of his sermon—and I can see him circling the field, looking for a runway to lay that baby down—"Lastly...and in conclusion...and furthermore...and may God bless this truth to your hearts," which being interpreted means, "I don't have a clue as to how to finish this thing off."

Between the introduction and the conclusion you need illustrations in your spoken message (as well as actual visual aids, which should be included whenever possible). These are windows that let in light so that your hearers can say, "Aha, I see it!" Don't pull illustrations from someone else; get them yourself right from the lifestyle of the people you're teaching. Talk in terms of where they are, which means you've got to know them well and be sensitive to what's on their minds and hearts right now.

As I disciple a layman, one of my favorite pastimes is to take him out to breakfast or lunch and ask him a simple question: "What are you struggling with? What are the problems you face down at the office?" I don't talk. I just listen, and I write down as much as I can. People like him are my teachers.

Never forget: A good communicator is *receptor*-sensitive.

That's why I love working with laymen and laywomen—business people, homemakers, carpenters, plumbers, doctors, lawyers, professional football players—people who, after being taught the truth, will express it in their own words, in the medium of expression with which they're comfortable. They make the truth their own personal property. The message is translated into their own vocabulary. Their words are not the same as their teacher's words.

So the test of communication is not what you as the teacher say, but what your students say; not what you think, but what they think; not what you feel, but what they feel; not what you're doing, but what they're doing.

2. *Presentation* involves, among other things, enunciation—speaking clearly so people understand exactly what you're saying.

I was raised in the northeastern part of our country, where we tend to neglect three essentials to enunciation—the lips, the teeth, and the tongue. Later, as a student at Wheaton College, I took private music lessons. The professor started garbling her instructions to me, and I thought, "This lady's got problems." Then one day it dawned on me: She was talking to me the way I talked to her. So I started enunciating, and my peers on campus told me, "Howie, for the first time we're beginning to understand what you're talking about."

Another factor is the volume of your voice. If you have a large class, always imagine that the guy in the back row has a hearing aid and the battery just went out. This is particularly true at the start of each class time. This is not to say you should shout, though I must admit I occasionally wish some speakers would—it might convince me they're interested in what they're talking about. There will also be times when, for emphasis, you'll want to drop down and speak very softly.

Another pointer: Vary both your pitch—don't be a Johnny-one-note—and your speed. Pick them up when you want to convey excitement. Bring them down when you're emphasizing a major point.

Distractions

If I had my way, every person who wanted to learn to teach would be required to teach preschoolers first. It's definitely a liberal arts education.

You go in with your outline firmly in mind—

    I. Purpose of prayer

II. Power of prayer

III. Product of prayer

and you get started. You throw in a little Greek to impress them: *euchomai*, *proseuchomai*, *erōtaō*. Suddenly a little bird lands on the ledge outside the window, and—boom—the whole class jumps up and deserts you to take a closer look.

Of course, adults do the same thing. They don't actually get up and leave. They just sit there politely and shake their heads, occasionally the wrong way. But the truth of the matter is that their minds are often a thousand miles away. Distractions are usually the cause.

Distractions come in two forms. Some are within the individual hearer and can't be controlled:

...the woman who was too stressed to sleep last night;

...the man whose wife is dying of cancer;

...another who was served notice this week by his company that they can get along without him—and he's putting two children through college;

...the couple who walked in with their Christian faces on after a knock-down-drag-out fight on the way to church (both are now mentally sharpening their weapons for the next round).

All this is severe static on the line. You can't do anything about most of it, except to understand that it will be there.

Other distractions you can usually control, such as the room temperature, which no one ever notices unless it's too hot or too cold. Or the setup of the room. Try getting to class early and rearranging the chairs. That may blow the minds of a few saints ("We're facing the wrong direction—he's gone to liberalism!"), but to others it will communicate that something different's going on today, something that could be exciting.

How about having your visual aids in order? There's nothing funnier than watching the average children's teacher operate the flannelboard when she hasn't taken time to arrange the figures in proper order. "Today we have the story of Abraham," she says—but where's Abraham? Off she goes on an archaeological expedition to find him. Or she has the board at the wrong angle when she's telling the story of Joshua. She gets almost to the climax of the story and—slam, the whole thing comes down. The kids roar, and the teacher thinks, "These godless kids!" No, they're not godless, they're godly. They have a sense of humor just as God does, and they love to laugh.

Then there are the times you're speaking to a large group as an usher comes quietly down the side aisle with a message for someone on the platform…and EVERYBODY watches him. You know what I'm going to do the next time that happens to me? I'm going to stop and say, "Ladies and gentlemen, there's a man walking down the side aisle. Keep your eyes on him. He is now approaching the platform. Watch him carefully. He's now handing a note to Brother Gumball. Brother Gumball is now whispering a few words to him. The man is now walking away from the platform. And there he goes…back up the aisle." Then I'll return to where I left off in the message.

Eliminate as many of those distractions as possible.

Feedback

Here's a final step in the communication process, and don't miss this or you miss it all: Get feedback.

As the teacher I want to find out what the learners know, how they feel, and what they're doing.

I've got to get the learners to tell me what they're learning. So I may ask them questions. The number one question, in one form or another, is "Do you understand?" And if the answer is "No, I don't have a clue," you've got to go back to square one.

(Wouldn't it be great in our churches if people would simply stand up when they didn't understand what the speaker was trying to communicate, and say, "Wait a minute. I have no idea what you're talking about"? It would guarantee no one would go to sleep!)

I can also get feedback by asking them to write it in their own words: "Tell me how you can apply this in your sphere of influence."

Or I can ask, "Do *you* have any questions?" And they will ask revealing questions that show if I have failed to put in a form they can understand what I wanted them to know, to feel, and to do. I'll realize the holes in my communication.

At the seminary I'll bring together a small group of students at the end of a term and ask them, "What needs to be changed in this course? What did you like? What didn't you like? What didn't make sense? Don't tell me what I want to hear; tell me what I *need* to hear." And they'll tell me.

I once spoke in a Sunday evening service at a church on the West coast. The place was jammed to the doors. Before I went in, the pastor said, "Dr. Hendricks, I forgot to tell you: Once we're inside you'll notice a table on the left. Tonight you'll see seated there a plumber, a medical doctor, a housewife, a high-school student, and a missionary home on furlough. After you get through speaking, they're going to ply you with questions. You don't mind, do you?" "Now he tells me," I thought.

I've never been asked such perceptive questions as I was asked that night. They punched holes in my presentation with questions that reflected the deepest needs out there in the audience. The panel was there to make sure I spoke in terms of those needs.

If you're willing to listen to feedback like that, there's no way you can keep from improving as a teacher.

Feedback brings us back where we started: The concept-feeling-action is being translated into words. But this time it's not *your* concept-feeling-action and *your* words, but theirs—the learners'.

They aren't parrots who simply spill out exactly what you have told them. Rather, they *understand*, just as you have understood. They *feel deeply about it*, as you have felt. And like you, they're allowing the truth to affect their actions in a significant way.

ow can the teacher's manner fail to be earnest and inspiring when his subject matter is so rich in radiant reality?

JOHN MILTON GREGORY

THE LAW OF THE HEART

Teaching that impacts is not head to head, but heart to heart.

That's the Law of the Heart, and it's true as long as you understand the biblical meaning of *heart.*

It's one of those quicksilver words, and kind of mushy. We tend to use the word imprecisely today, but the Old Testament writers never did.

Deuteronomy 6:4–6 is one passage that reveals the scriptural context for the word. Moses said, "Hear, O Israel: The LORD our God, the LORD is one. Love the LORD your God with all your *heart* and with all your soul and with all your strength. These commandments that I give you today are to be upon your *hearts.*"

To the Hebrews, *heart* embraced the totality of human personality—one's intellect, one's emotions, one's will.

So the process of teaching is that of one total personality transformed by the supernatural grace of God, reaching out to transform other personalities by the same grace. What a privilege!

It's the simplest thing in the world to take only the head trip. Taking the way of the heart is much more difficult. But it's also more profitable. In fact, it's life-changing.

Character—Compassion—Content

Socrates summarized the essence of communication with three fascinating concepts that he called *ethos, pathos,* and *logos. Ethos* embraced character. *Pathos* embraced compassion. *Logos* embraced content.

Ethos, as Socrates thought of it, meant establishing the credibility of the teacher—his credentials. He understood that who you are is far more impor-tant than what you say or do, because it *determines* what you say and do. Who you are as a person is your greatest leverage as a speaker, a persuader, a communicator. You must be attractive to those who would learn from you. They must trust you, and the more they trust you, the more you communicate to them.

Pathos, or compassion, concerns how the teacher arouses the passions of his hearers and massages their emotions. Socrates knew that your emotions must run in the direction of your action. That's the secret to motivation, because God created us as emotional, feeling beings.

Socrates knew also that speakers and teachers need content, and he called it—interestingly enough—*logos*, the same Greek word used of Jesus Christ in John 1: "In the beginning was the *logos*, the Word. And the *logos* became flesh, and pitched his tent among us, and we beheld his glory—the glory of the Father's one and only Son, full of grace and truth." When God wanted to communicate with us, he wrapped his message in a person. That's exactly what we are called to do.

The *logos* concept therefore involves the marshaling of your evidence. It engages the mind and gives understanding. It provides reasons for the action you want the learners to take so they see how logical and reasonable that action is.

As a teacher you can, of course, teach without character, without compassion, without content. But think with me what that does to the learner.

For the teacher's *character* is what produces the learner's *confidence*. When I see the quality of your life, I know you have something significant as a teacher to contribute to me. I can trust you. I know you wouldn't lie to me.

This trust factor, this confidence in you, is the greatest commodity you have going for you in communication. Never do anything to shred it. It's the hardest thing to build back.

Understand that the basis of all effective communication emanates from within. Ask yourself periodically, "What kind of a person am I?"

Second, it's your *compassion* that produces the learner's *motivation*. If I sense you love me, I'll be eager to do all kinds of things you want me to do.

Why did the disciples follow Jesus? It's simple: He loved them. The gospels tell us, "When Christ saw the multitudes, he was moved with compassion for them." Men and women and youth and children are all drawn to a person who loves them.

What response do people evoke in you? Do they bother you? Challenge you? Do you like people, or do they threaten you?

Third, it's your *content* that produces the learner's *perception*. You as the teacher have seen it—now I as the learner see it. I understand it, I have discovered it. It is mine, woven into the fabric of my life.

The greatest communicators—the greatest teachers—are not necessarily the people up front with high visibility. They are the people who have great heart. They communicate *as* a total person, and they communicate *to* the total person of their hearers.

The Teaching–Learning Process

Think for a moment about what teaching and learning really are.

Teaching is *causing*. Causing what? Causing people to learn. That's the simplest definition I know.

There's a very essential relationship between teaching and learning. It's the *teaching-learning* process, and notice the hyphen. These words are inseparable. If the learner does not learn, we have not taught.

Now please note: Teaching is what *you* do; learning is what your students do. We have preserved that distinction in the English language. We never say, "I learned him," because that's impossible. The student must do the learning; all the teacher can do is teach.

So the focus in teaching is primarily on what you as the teacher do, and the focus in learning is primarily on what the student does. But we test the effectiveness of your teaching not by what you do, but by what the student does as a result of what you do.

The simplest definition I know of learning is this: Learning is *change*.

Essentially, learning means a change in your thinking, a change in your feeling, a change in your behavior. Learning means that a change takes place in the mind, in the emotions, and in the will.

When someone has learned, that person will have changed. Paul looks at this in Romans 8:29—"For those God foreknew he also predestined to be conformed to the likeness of his Son." Underline that word *conformed* in your Bible.

You know the process. You take some Jell-O, mix it with water, pour the mixture into a mold, and place it in the refrigerator. Hours later you bring it out, turn it upside down on a plate, and there you have it. Paul says, "You are predestined to be poured into the mold of Jesus Christ." What revolutionary change that calls for!

Just a few pages further, in Romans 12:2, we see Paul using the same word again: "Do not *conform* any longer to the pattern of this world." Or as J. B. Phillips paraphrased it, "Don't let the world around you squeeze you into its own mold." Put these passages together and you see a divinely intended purpose: You are predestined to be poured into the mold of Jesus Christ—so don't let the world squeeze you into its mold, for these two processes are diametrically opposed.

And just how do we keep the world from squeeze-molding us? Paul answers, "Be transformed by the renewing of your mind." It's by *transforming*. A metamorphosis. It's not a transforming from without, but from within— "by the renewing of your mind. Then you will be able to test and approve what God's will is—his good, pleasing and perfect will."

Change. Radical change. Thus we are conformed to the likeness of God's Son.

So you come to your class and challenge them about discipleship. You take them to Luke 14 and other passages. And you say, "Do you want to change your life?"

"Oh sure," come the answers.

"Then throw it away."

"*Throw it away?*" someone exclaims. "But don't you know we only go around once in life? You gotta grab all the gusto you can." It's interesting that people who would never touch a drop of beer can be shot through with that philosophy. Exposure to massive doses of worldly thinking squeezes us into the world's mold. But we open the way to change when we turn away from that and let the living truth of God move into our minds, our emotions, and our behavior.

Yet so often we see no responsibility in connection to our knowing. We overload the circuits with knowledge, and fail to teach people that when God reveals himself to you, you are responsible. The ball is in your court.

By virtue of reading this book, believe me, you are in debt. God will hold you responsible for what you do with what you have been exposed to.

Where Learning Begins

All learning begins at the feeling level.

People accept what they feel disposed to accept, and they reject what they feel disposed to reject.

If their attitude is positive, they tend to embrace what they hear. If their attitude is negative, they tend to walk away from it.

If I have negative feelings about you, I will reject what you're saying because I reject you.

But if I like you—and if I know you're interested in me—you can get me to do the most incredible things in all the world. And there's a good possibility I'm also going to like your Lord, who made you the way you are.

No one cares what you know until they know that you care.

What about those you teach? Are they receptive or hostile?

Perhaps as they listen to you, they're thinking, "I've heard that before; and furthermore, I suspect you're just as much a fake as the last guy who fed me that line." If so, you've got your work cut out for you.

It might help, as you come before them, to picture each individual out there with a gun in his hand. Your task is to get them to take the guns out of their hands and lay them down. You do that by your relationship with them—by establishing rapport so that your audience is free to interact with you on the subject you're teaching.

You do it with *heart*.

Think what would happen to the average teenager in your class next Sunday if you caught him going out the door, drew him next to you and said, "Hey man, I just want you to know I'm on your team. I'm praying for you. If you ever need any help, give me a call, okay? I'm for you."

He would never forget who you are. How do I know? I was that kid.

I can go back to my church in Philadelphia, and they'll hug me and say, "Oh Howard, we're so proud of you." But to some of them I've occasionally felt like saying, "Really, you didn't help at all." Not many of the people there ever saw me as anything other than the brat from Seventh Street. But how I thank God for those few who *did* see me as something else! I thank God every single day I live for those people who somehow cared enough for me to tell me, "It's okay, Howie. We're with you. We love you. We're praying for you."

So let's say you're teaching a class of junior-high kids, and you have one kid who hates being there, but he's shotgunned into coming.

You can't ignore his attitude. So you tell him, "Hey, Phil, could I drop by tomorrow after school so we can go have a Coke?" The next day you sit down and talk, and eventually you say, "It's really bad news that you've got to come to Sunday school, isn't it?"

"Yeah."

"In fact, if you had your choice, you'd never be there, right?"

"That's right."

"I just want you to know it's great having you there. It's such a pleasure knowing you. Thanks for showing up. But I understand. I was a teenager once, though I know that's hard for you to believe. I know where you're coming from. But that's okay, I love you anyway."

Watch what happens to his attitude. He's still shotgunned into coming to Sunday school, but you as the teacher are no longer part of the problem. You're both on the same team.

Or you're teaching small children, and little Joanne comes in wearing new shoes. If you don't take notice of them right away, do you know when you're going to hear about them? In the middle of your Bible story. You'll get right to the climax, every kid's eyes will be wide as saucers, and suddenly little Joanne will jump up and exclaim, "Did you see my *new shoes?*" (Of course, if you were as close to your shoes as little Joanne is to hers, you'd talk more about them too.)

That's why when she walks in, you say, "Hi, Joanne. Wow, look at those new shoes!" And in your story you somehow find a place to talk about someone getting new shoes—"*just like Joanne's!*" She's right with you all the way.

Never Forget the Facts

I'm not saying content is unimportant.

Every now and then someone says to me, "You know, Hendricks, it really makes no difference *what* you believe. The important thing is *how* you believe." But that's biblical nonsense. It makes all the difference in the world what you believe, because what you believe determines how you behave. To be sure, you can believe correctly and not behave correctly. But you cannot consistently behave correctly *unless* you believe correctly.

You see, God has spoken, and he hasn't stuttered. The Bible is a revelation, not a riddle.

People say to me, "You know, I can't figure this book out. I think the Lord's playing games with me." They're afraid they'll lose the game, and when they get to heaven God will gloat, "Aha! You didn't understand it!"

I tell them that God is far more concerned than we are that we understand his book. But we understand it by *studying* it. It is not a rabbit's foot. You can't get miraculous changes in your life by rubbing it.

Has it occurred to you that when God shaped his message in his Book, he did it with the conscious intention of speaking directly to you, on this very day near the end of the twentieth century?

God wants to communicate with us, and he has written his message in a

Book that contains everything we need for now and eternity. This is our given. This is our message.

Allow me to remind you that Christianity is based not merely on experience (though it produces an experience), but on historical fact.

Paul reminded us of this in 1 Corinthians 15. What is the essence of the gospel? Paul said it is four historical facts:

Christ died.

He was buried.

He rose again.

He appeared to certain people.

How do we know Christ died? Because he was buried. How do we know he rose again? Because he appeared to certain people.

So content is critically important from a biblical point of view. We've got to know the truth God has revealed. Never forget the facts of the word of God. But that's not the end of the ball game. There's more. There's the feeling level, the emotions; and there's the level of the will—action, behavior.

Until the mind has been changed, and the emotions have been changed, and the will has been changed, biblical teaching and learning have not taken place.

Be a Person of Impact

I hope you're thinking, "Big deal, Hendricks, but so what? This is great truth, but how do I translate it into my teaching?"

I'll give you three things you can take and run with, if you want to be a person of impact. No one reading this book is incapable of doing these three things.

1. We've mentioned this before, and it's worth repeating: *Know your students.* The more you know of their needs, the better able you are to meet them.

This takes commitment of course, and it takes time, and that's where we lose a lot of teachers. But there's no magic formula. Good teaching has a price tag: You've got to be willing to pour out your life.

It means getting personally involved with your students, both in and out of class, both formally and informally. It means coming to class early and staying late just to talk with them. It means inviting them into your home.

Some of us professional teachers are educated beyond our intelligence. A typical college professor today comes to class prepared to the hilt. He loves the subject and can talk on it at the drop of a hat. But after class is over he disappears, and you won't see him till the next class. If you want to catch him to talk with him, you have to trip him on his way out.

My wife speaks frequently at women's conferences. We try to coordinate our ministry schedules so we can travel together, but now and then she's away without me. Then I'll call up one of the single men's dorms at the seminary and ask if I can spend the weekend there. "Are you kidding?" they'll say.

"No. And promise you won't short-sheet me." (You wouldn't believe what they try to do to me.)

So I'll be there for the weekend and have the time of my life, talking for hours with ten or fifteen guys at a time crowded into a dorm room. It's a zoo, but it's exciting.

Some of us are in a dream world, not really knowing where our students are. So I dare you to flow into their lives.

You can impress people at a distance. But you can impact them only up close.

And the closer you are to them, the greater and more permanent the impact.

Ever let people see you when your guard is down? I once asked some students over to watch a televised Cowboy-Redskins football game. On one play I overexcitedly banged my fist and let fly my wristwatch—which ended up in pieces. "Ah, he's human," one of the guys said. Yes, disgustingly so.

We usually set up all our ducks in a row and only *then* let people in to see us. But what they really need is to see you when you're discouraged or when you've lost your temper. Then they won't deny your humanity but realize you're cut from the same cloth they are.

2. *Earn the right to be heard.* You can't walk out on the street and tell the first guy you meet that you know what his problem is. He'll probably give you a portion of his mind that he can't afford to lose. Even if you *do* know what his problem is, I can guarantee you won't get through to him.

Credibility always precedes communication.

That's why I'm convinced that some of the most ordinary people in our churches are having the most extraordinary ministries, because they have earned the right. They're not the people you see on the major platforms, but they're the people who change lives—and our celebrity society has never figured that out.

So win a hearing.

3. *Be willing to become vulnerable before your students.* Let them know what you're struggling with and what you've struggled with for years.

If your class is children, tell them what you struggled with when you were their age. They'll latch on to it and love it. If they're teenagers, let them know you were a teenager once and had your share of problems. (If you don't believe you did, ask someone who knew you back then; they'll give you some data.)

One of the greatest responses I get from students is when I mention the problem I had with depression. They can identify easily with that, but not with my successes.

Remember, most people will tend to see you in terms of where you are now, rather than in light of where you've come from and what you've gone through. They didn't see the process. Yet, by the grace of God, you've come a long way. So get the picture of how to pass on to others what God has taught you through those stretching experiences and those agonizing failures—experiences that made you the person you are.

he nature of

mind, as far as we can under-

stand it, is that of a power or

force actuated by motives. The

striking clock may sound in

the ear, and the passing object

may paint its image in the

eyes, but the inattentive mind

neither hears nor sees.

JOHN MILTON GREGORY

6

The Law of Encouragement

Inside the box at the bottom of this page are all the secrets of motivation. Do you believe me? The box is locked, but fortunately I have the key, so let's take a look inside.

The first thing I pull out is a small paper bag filled with interesting rocks. A seven-year-old boy spent three hours on a Saturday morning collecting them. No one told him to do this. It wasn't an assignment for any course. But for some reason or other, he chose to do it. Why do you think he did?

The second thing I take from the box is a well-worn baby care book—with all kinds of stains on it and pages falling out. My wife and I reared four kids on it. No one ever made that book assigned reading for her, yet she turned to it again and again. Why do you think she did?

Next is a packet of Scripture memory verse cards. Have you ever started a Bible memory program? If you did, why? And if you started, have you ever quit? Why?

The next item is a certain IRS tax information booklet from the federal government. Ever had your daily devotions in one of those? Exciting—more fun than having leprosy. But someone said to me once, "Hendricks, if you read this, it will save you six hundred dollars." Do you think I read it? Yes I did—and it saved me six hundred dollars and then some.

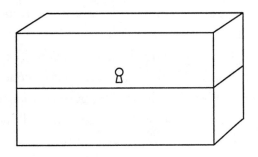

Now I pull out a uniform shirt from my son Bill's days with the Christian Service Brigade, an organization like the Boy Scouts but with a Christian orientation. On one pocket are four award patches—and you wouldn't believe how hard he worked to get them. Each patch cost only thirty-five cents, but how much do you think they meant to Bill? Who could even put a price tag on them?

I think I've read everything written on how to motivate people. But I've never found any successful method that isn't represented by the items in that box—concepts like *ownership, curiosity, meeting needs, usefulness, challenge, recognition, approval.*

The number one problem in education today is the failure to motivate learners...to get them off the dime and into action.

The longer I teach, the more convinced I am that a person's MQ—his Motivation Quotient—is more important than his IQ.

I've seen students who by graduation time are highly qualified to be utterly useless. Their problem isn't lack of ability. We determined they had ability before we admitted them as students. No, their problem was lack of application. There was nothing to capture and direct their ability and energy. They were not motivated to apply themselves.

The Law of Encouragement is this: *Teaching tends to be most effective when the learner is properly motivated.*

Underline the word *properly* in that definition, because it tells us there's such a thing as improper motivation—illegitimate motivation that can bring devastating results.

One form of it is what I call lollipop motivation: "Son, behave yourself in church this morning, and I'll buy you an ice-cream cone." Or, "Memorize two hundred verses of Scripture, and we'll send you to camp for a week." Now those sound good, and they can make students do good things. But it's altogether possible that those good things will not have good results.

When I was youth director in a church in Illinois, a boy in the junior department had memorized six hundred verses word perfectly. We even had him on a Christian radio program and tested him on the air.

Later we were told someone apparently was stealing money from the junior-department offering each Sunday. A committee was appointed to investigate, and—you guessed it—the kid who knew the six hundred verses was the culprit.

I called him into my office and repeated to him a verse of Scripture (which, by the way, he told me I misquoted). I said, "Do you see any connection between that verse of Scripture and your stealing from the offering?"

"No," he said at first. And then, "Well, maybe there is."

"What do you think is the connection?"

"I got caught," he said.

So doing good things does not ensure good results. It's all determined by the motivation.

Another improper motivation is guilt. That's another reason many people memorize Scripture: *I can't be a first-class Christian if I don't memorize these verses*. In fact, this is probably one of the most common motivations some Christian communicators use. They keep piling the guilt higher and higher, and the people keep making the formations and salivating when you ring the bell. But all for the wrong reasons.

Yet another improper motivation involves deceit—intentional or unintentional. If I told you I knew a success formula and convinced you that if you tried it immediately, it would totally revolutionize your life, you probably would give it a shot…but only once. It had better work the first time, or that would be the last thing you'd listen to from me.

So friend, let's stop promising people more than Christianity promises them, more than the Scriptures promise them. Don't say, "If you come to Christ, all your problems will be solved." That's how people get disillusioned. Sure, Christ will meet their needs, but not according to your script, or in your time, or in your way.

I'm leading people to Christ who are discovering they have problems they never knew they had. Like the guy who didn't know his marriage needed work until he came to Jesus Christ and began to study the Scriptures and God said to him, "I want you to love your wife as Christ loved the church." Then he knew: It's a whole new experience.

So be careful what you tell people as a tool for motivation.

Awareness of Need

There are two levels of motivation. The first is extrinsic motivation—motivation from without. The second is more significant—intrinsic motivation, which comes from within.

Your task in all extrinsic motivation is to trigger intrinsic motivation. You wish you could crawl inside a student, rummage around, find his hot button, and press it. But you can't. You have to work on the outside to get something to happen on the inside.

We can see something of how God accomplishes this internal motivation in a verse of Scripture I suspect you have committed to memory—Romans 12:1.

It begins, "Therefore…"—and whenever you see a *therefore* in Scripture, you want to find out what it's "there for." Paul continues: "by the mercies of God." What mercies? The mercies he has just spent eleven chapters spelling out in detail. So on the basis of God's mercies, on the basis of what God has done for you, Paul says, "I urge you to offer your bodies as living sacrifices."

My deep conviction is that one of the reasons we are not getting higher commitment to discipleship in the evangelical community is that we ask people to *do things for God*. Yet God never asks you to do anything for him until he fully informs you of what he has done for you. When finally you are gripped by all he has done for you, your most logical, reasonable, intelligent, and natural response in return is to give everything you've got—your mind, your emotions, your will—to his lordship. Now you're internally motivated and on your way to maturity.

We have too many parents and teachers who think their primary goal with a child is to rear a good boy or a good girl. But their job is to rear a good *man* or a good *woman*—that is, a self-starter who's internally loaded. We have too many people at age forty-six who are still good boys and girls.

As a teacher—a motivator—you want to help people develop into self-starters. You want them to do what they do, not because you ask them or twist their arm, but because they themselves have chosen to do it.

One of the best ways to trigger this choice is to help the learner become aware of his need.

Suppose I offer you lessons in public speaking. You answer, "Well, Hendricks, I don't think I'm really interested; you see, I'm really not that bad of a speaker."

"Good," I say. "I'd like to have you speak at our businessmen's luncheon next Thursday. We'll have about three or four hundred men there, mostly non-Christians, and I'd like you to give a three-minute testimony."

You can't get out of it now. "Uhhh...sure, sure. Three minutes?"

"Yep. That means three times sixty seconds."

"Ha, ha...sure, of course."

Next Thursday you get up and look out on all those people, and you're paralyzed. You grip your notes as if you're afraid they'll fly away. You tell a joke and forget the punch line. You start your testimony and put the end at the beginning. The rest is a daze. You can't see anyone past the third row. It's a disaster. Finally you sit down.

"Guess I went over a little," you whisper.

"Only nine minutes," I say. "By the way, how would you like me to give you some lessons in public speaking?"

"When do we start?"

The need has become a *felt* need. That's why much of your method in teaching should be exposing your students to real-life experiences.

For a number of years I taught a course in counseling. A student once came up after class and said, "Prof, have you got anything a little more challenging?"

"Yeah," I said, "I think I can find something." I called up a friend at the juvenile delinquency center in Dallas and told him, "I've got a student who needs an education."

"I've got the picture," he said. So I sent the student out. They put him in a cell with a fourteen-year-old kid billed on twenty-six major counts. The state was just waiting for him to grow up so they could put him away permanently.

He was sitting with his feet propped up on the window sill when my student was led in and the door clanked shut behind him. The kid turned and said, "Every day they send somebody in here with a different line. So what's yours?"

"Prof," the student told me later, "I lost it right there." He came back to class ready to learn more.

I once met another seminary student on his way to give an evangelistic talk at a fraternity house on the university campus. He asked for my prayers.

"What do you want me to pray for?" I asked.

"Pray they won't go for my jugular," he said.

I told him I was going to pray they did exactly that.

The next day he said, "The Lord answered your prayer." They shredded him. But today he has one of the best ministries to college students in America, and he looks back to that day in the fraternity as the point when he really got the picture—when he discovered how much he didn't know.

Good Training

You motivate people by correctly structuring their training experience.

Training involves four major stages. The first is the *telling* stage, and we're usually strongest here. I always recommend in this stage that the content be recorded both in writing and on tape. Don't make learners depend on just one exposure to the content, but put it in a form they can review repeatedly. Only then will they really begin to catch on. Our research has shown, incidentally, that for effective learning, women are more likely to read books, and men are more likely to listen to tapes—though of course there are exceptions.

The next stage is the *showing* stage. You provide a model. What does it look like? Flesh it out. Let them watch you out there in the alligator pits, sweating it out, relating truth to your life. When they see it in action, they'll say, "Hey, that's what I want."

We often miss it here. In our Sunday school teacher training courses we say, "Come next week for a very important session on storytelling." Next week they come, and the instructor gets up and says, "Stories are very important. Jesus told stories. All great teachers have told stories. There are five major parts to a story, and here they are...." Then he comes to the end of the presentation and says, "Anyone have a question?" But who would? They wouldn't know a story if they fell over it. "Come back next week for another exciting teacher training session," we say—and they stay away in droves.

Stages three and four involve *doing*—but in different ways: first in a *controlled* situation, then in *uncontrolled*, real-life situations.

I've never heard of a correspondence course in swimming. No, you learn to swim by swimming, not by reading books and not by watching the pros go up and down the pool. You've got to get wet.

I used to send my students to observe university law school classes taught by one of the most brilliant teachers I've known, a man who produced more successful trial lawyers than any other law professor in Texas. He was known for being a little rough, but the students knew he loved them and would devote all his expertise and skill to help them.

He set up his trial law classes like a courtroom with the prosecution on one side and the defense on the other, with one student as the judge and others making up the jury. Everyone got in the act.

The trial began, and soon the professor would storm down the center aisle, railing against the prosecution: "You don't mean to tell me you're going to try the case like that, are you?" After exposing their weaknesses one by one, he would whip around and challenge the students on the other side: "Do you know what I would do with a defense that shoddy? I'd murder it."

When class time was over, he would say with a wink, "Do you want to know how to win this case? Follow me." Across campus he would go with twenty students behind him, and together over coffee they would talk about it.

I once asked him his philosophy of education. He said, "I'd rather have my students lose in here and win out there than to win in here and lose out there."

What about us? Are our students winning inside the church but losing like crazy in the real world?

I think I've taken seven courses in personal evangelism—I thought about that one day and counted them up. Honesty compels me to say not one of them did a blessed thing for me.

In one course in college we memorized a list of Scripture verses matched with common objections people have to the gospel. Then they sent us to Union Station in Chicago. The first guy I talked with brought up an objection that wasn't on the list. And I was hung!

Of course, back in my student days in college and seminary I had all the answers to ineffective teaching. I used to sit in class and think, "Man, this is sad. This has to be the weakest course I've had yet. And I'm paying for it!" I had a root of bitterness you wouldn't believe.

Then one day I expressed my feelings to a visiting missionary, and he said, "Howie, I've got your problem. You are destructively critical, not constructively critical. When you're in class, try drawing a line down the middle of your notepaper. On one side, keep your class notes as you normally do. On the other, write down what you would do differently if you were teaching the course."

Not a bad suggestion. And because I followed it, I can look back and see how in those classes I formed and shaped my philosophy of theological education. I had no idea I would ever be teaching in a seminary, but I knew there had to be a better way to do it than what I was often given.

When I taught homiletics at the seminary, we had a lot of fun with a certain assignment I often gave early in the course: "Come up with an illustration—any one you want, illustrating any point—and come to the next class prepared to give it orally."

The next class time came around, and a few students were shrinking in their chairs hoping I wouldn't see them.

"Okay, man," I would say to one of them, "you're on."

"Me, Prof?"

"You."

He would get up reluctantly, start telling his story, and halt. "Good night, Prof, I forgot the ending. Let me sit down."

"Naw, you can't sit down. Anybody here want him to sit down?" The class would give a chorus of noes. "Nobody wants you to sit down."

Finally he remembered the rest. The class applauded, and he sat down and smiled.

"Is this the first time you've done that?"

"Very first time, Prof."

"Did you enjoy it?"

"No," he would laugh, "it was horrible."

I could name students like that who now are known internationally for their speaking ministries, men whom you celebrate. But you should have heard the first message they gave in class. Painful!

Of course, I break out in a cold sweat when I remember having to greet people as they left the first church service I ever preached at. "Oh, Lord, why?" I thought. I wished there were a trapdoor behind the pulpit so I could disappear. "Oh, Howard, that was wonderful," the dear people said, and I knew they were lying. But that's where we all have to start.

Another mark of good training is giving people *responsibility with accountability*. Our problem in the churches is that we don't do that. The United States government takes multimillion-dollar planes and puts them in the hands of kids nineteen years old, and when those same kids come to church, we won't even let them take up the offering.

The more you put into something, the more you appreciate it.

The greater the investment, the greater the interest.

A leading authority on training tells me that some of the best training in all the world is taking place in the cults.

One Sunday morning I was home recovering from surgery. Two nicely dressed men who didn't know me from Adam knocked at my door. (Evangelicals never think of doing evangelistic calling on Sunday mornings, even though it's the most likely time for pagans to be home.) One was older, one younger. I invited them in, and we got into quite a conversation.

We were looking at several Bible passages, and they frequently said, "Now the Greek says so-and-so."

"The Greek?" I said. "What in the world does Greek have to do with it?"

"Well, Mr. Hendricks," said the younger man, "apparently you don't know much about the New Testament. It was written in Greek."

"Fascinating. Do you read Greek?"

"Well, yes, it's part of our training."

"Good," I said. I reached for my Greek New Testament and handed it to him. He turned every color of the rainbow.

Pretty soon the older man tried to bail him out, but I began refuting their statements—"You see, the Greek here doesn't mean at all what you say it means." So they got up to leave.

And where did they go? Next door? No, not immediately. They were too smart for that. This was a trainable, teachable moment. I watched the two of them go a little further down the street and stop, and they talked for an hour. The older man, the trainer, was no doubt telling the trainee how to keep out of that kind of rhubarb the next time.

Only then did they go to my next-door neighbor. I asked him the next day, "Jim, which one talked?"

"The younger one," he said. Of course. He was in training.

The Personal Touch

Ever been in a courtroom where a will is being read? The reader is mumbling his way over the legal jargon, and everyone else in the room is half asleep—everyone, that is, except the person named in the will as the beneficiary.

The application: When your teaching has the learner's name written all over it—when he sees that, in effect, his name occurs throughout the Book, and it's *personal*—it will make a big difference in his level of motivation.

I've been teaching for more than thirty-five years in the same school, and it's quite humbling to consider the ministry impact today of some of the students God has marked through my life. I think the reason God has used me is that, by his grace, the Holy Spirit has developed in me an incurable confidence in his ability to change people.

I trust the Spirit has given you that same confidence, because if you don't have it, your impact will always be limited. The Spirit of God wants to use you as his motivational tool working externally upon the learner, while he is at work internally.

Some of the best motivators I know never work in a classroom. They are teachers without the label—men and women who are doing discipleship and changing the lives and the perspectives of other people. Why? Because they are willing to flow into other people's lives.

I'm convinced that everyone—no exception—can be motivated to learn.

But not at the same time…and not by the same person…and not in the same way.

The timing is crucial. Teaching is the assembling of a time bomb in a classroom, marked for explosion at a later date and in a different location.

That's why you need to walk by faith to be a good teacher, and you need a lot of patience.

And *you* are not God's answer to every individual. That's what the body of Christ is all about. You can reach people I couldn't touch with a twenty-foot pole, and someone else can reach others whom neither you nor I could.

Creative Motivation

The people in my church had a motto: "Go ye into all the world and take pictures."

Before we went to the Orient, they told us—as they tell anyone who travels—"Please take pictures." So we did, and we showed them to people when we returned.

"Now," I told Jeanne, "we move into Step Two." After the next Sunday night service, we invited over three medical doctors from our fellowship. There in our home I began showing them the pictures. "Here's one of a clinic out in a remote tribal area."

"How did the clinic get started?" they asked.

"By a professor of surgery who walked out of Harvard Medical School one day and told them to hang it on their beak; he was going where the action was."

I continued, "Now this next shot is the pharmacy." They were looking at the pharmacy interior—nothing but empty shelves.

"The pharmacy?" they said. "Where are the pharmaceuticals?"

"I don't know. That's what pharmacies are like back there."

"Wait a minute," one of them said. "How can you have a pharmacy without pharmaceuticals?"

"I don't know. But that's what they have." I went on to the next shot. We continued through the other photos, but their first question when we got to the end was: "Now, how in the world can you have a pharmacy without pharmaceuticals?"

Since that night, these doctors and a number of other people have sent millions of dollars worth of pharmaceuticals to places where they're needed around the world. How did they get hooked? The same way you as a teacher can hook anyone: Once you get to know your students, let them get to know you, and then build creatively on that knowledge.

And since God motivates people in different ways, we need to be creative and use a variety of methods.

I've had the privilege of teaching high-school students as well as adults of every age. I've taught professional career people and people who are under-privileged. I've taught groups of men and groups of women. I've taught doctors and lawyers, and I've taught children. And every one of these groups brings to the class a different set of abilities and a different set of interests that can be creatively harnessed.

Take teenagers, for example. "We can't get these kids excited about the word of God," I hear. But I don't believe that. Our problem is that we aren't willing enough to put our creative hooks into the areas of their interests and abilities.

We damn what they do and how they do it, rather than helping them develop alternatives. We should have learned by now never to *prohibit* without also *providing*; it's not enough to say, "Don't do that" without also saying, "You *can* do this."

We've got churches, for example, that crucify the kids because of the music they listen to. So I say to the adults, "Did you ever think of giving the kids an opportunity to use their music?"

They're aghast. "You mean *in the* CHURCH?"

"What do you think I mean—in a floor show downtown? Of course in the church." I've seen kids spend hours studying a Scripture passage to help them write a song for use in a ministry.

One of the things that most disturbs me about our evangelical community is our tendency to kill all creativity. The creativity is available, but we aren't providing outlets for it.

I know of a young musical genius who led his local symphony orchestra in a premiere performance while still a teenager, and who in his twenties was a guest conductor of the New York Philharmonic. He was the product of an evangelical church in his city, but that church *never once used his musical ability*. Today he's far removed from Jesus Christ.

The Power Unleashed

Some people tell me they have to prove the Bible is the word of God before they can have an impact in witnessing. I think they're tipping their hand. They've never unleashed that Book's power in daily life, letting it explode, exposing for all to see the radical and supernatural changes it can bring.

I'm asked over and over again, "How in the world do you get a person motivated?"

I answer, "When you sock someone with 20,000 volts of electricity, they don't turn to you and ask, 'Did you say something?' No, they *move*."

The key question is…Are *you* motivated?

Because motivated people become change agents.

In his book *The Crisis in the University*, Sir Walter Moberly cites the failure of evangelicals to penetrate university campuses with the gospel. To those who claim to follow Christ he says, "If one-tenth of what you believe is true, you ought to be ten times as excited as you are."

So many people in our churches have never become impassioned about the only thing ultimately worth getting impassioned about.

So if it's exciting…get excited!

*M*any teachers

go to their work either partly

prepared or wholly unprepared.

They are like messengers

without a message. They lack

entirely the power and enthusi-

asm necessary to produce the

fruits which we have a right to

look for from their efforts.

JOHN MILTON GREGORY

7

THE LAW OF READINESS

Before the race, runners stretch their muscles. Before the concert, the orchestra tunes up.

And there's a necessary preparation for both the learner and teacher as well.

The Law of Readiness is this: *The teaching-learning process will be most effective when both student and teacher are adequately prepared.* It highlights one of the great problems for teachers: Their students come to class cold.

Let's suppose you're teaching the Book of Isaiah in an adult Sunday school class. On a certain Sunday, a miracle has occurred: This morning you will actually get a full sixty minutes of pure teaching time (primarily because today they eliminated the "opening exercises"—a fascinating term, since most of them open little and exercise less).

So you've got a good hour ahead of you, and you begin by saying, "Would you please open your Bibles to Isaiah 27?" Immediately they're thinking,

"What's in Isaiah 27?"

"Who knows?"

And even, "Who cares?"

But you are a competent teacher, and you believe strongly in the value for our lives today of the message in Isaiah 27 You believe this chapter is a passage not only to be mastered, but to be mastered by.

Gradually the class begins to warm up to Isaiah 27. In fact, as the hour nears its end, they're beginning to think of questions. The passage you've explored has touched on various needs and problems in their lives. You have aroused their deep interest.

But the time is gone.

Class is over.

A week later, you walk in again and say, "Would you please open your Bibles to Isaiah 28?"

"What's in Isaiah 28?"

"Who knows?"

"Who cares?"

In this manner you work your way together through the book.

I want to propose an alternative approach, allowing you to get the best investment of time during that hour together: Do not think of the beginning of that class hour as the starting point for building interest in your subject. Instead, move the starting point back...so that by the time you get together, you are continuing to develop momentum. And by the time the class is over, the learners will have found answers to their questions and solutions to their problems and will be motivated to continue studying the passage on their own or with others.

Successful Assignments

This Law of Readiness provides the philosophical basis for...*assignments*. At the mere mention of the word, you may get a touch of paranoia: "But Brother Hendricks, you don't know my class! They won't do assignments! It's a waste of time."

I can guarantee you that as long as you don't give assignments, your students won't do them. But why don't you try them on for size? And allow me to give you some help.

Think again about a typical situation in class: *You* are thoroughly prepared, having drenched your mind in a certain passage of Scripture. *They*—or at least most of them—have not even read the passage once in the last six months. *You* come with enthusiasm, because in that passage you've found answers to questions and solutions to problems. *They* come with nothing.

The situation is usually the same with the Sunday morning sermon as well, and in my judgment this is the greatest weakness related to preaching: There's very little that prepares the hearers for it, and even less that follows up on it.

So think briefly about the value of assignments. I see three benefits in particular:

1. *They precipitate thinking.* Assignments are the mental warmup. They preheat the mind so it's working before class time begins.

2. *They provide a background,* a foundation on which to build. The student is aware of problems and issues concerning the passage and how it relates to his life. Questions have surfaced. Curiosity is rising.

3. *They develop habits of independent study*—and this is the most important benefit of good assignments. They encourage people to be not simply under God's word, but in it for themselves. And just watch what happens when they are!

Remember, your goal as a teacher is to develop lifelong learners. Your teaching time is to be a stimulus, not a substitute. And the only way you'll get people personally excited about the word of God is to motivate them to get in touch with this reality firsthand.

What are the characteristics of good assignments?

First, they must be creative, not simply busy work. That means you need a clear objective for the assignments; they must be designed with a purpose. This takes a lot of preparation time, because creative assignments don't just fall out of the air.

Second, they must be thought provoking. They should question more answers rather than answer more questions. Stretch the learners' minds. I know thinking is painful, but it can also be profitable when it's under the direction of the Spirit of God.

Third, assignments must be doable. Don't heap on an unrealistic load.

But if you've done your best to give assignments that are creative, thought provoking, and doable, what do you do in class if—for whatever reason—the students haven't done them?

A simple solution: Do an assignment in class, right then and there. Write a thought-provoking question on the board, then have them read through a selected passage that sheds light on it. (Be sure to follow that order—raise the question first, then read the passage—so they know what they're searching for.)

Another approach: Tap their experiences. Ask what problems they're facing now at home, on the job, at school. I tried this in a couples class about which I had been warned, "These people won't talk in class, and they won't do assignments." Won't, won't, won't.

"Thanks for the information," I said. Then I took a stack of three-by-five cards to the first class I taught, passed them out, and said, "You know, I have a lot of confidence in you people. I know you come from a variety of backgrounds, you're involved in a number of businesses and activities and so on. So I want you to take one of these cards—but don't put your name on it—and write down your answer to this question: If you knew you could get answers for any concern in your life right now, no matter what, which three would you most want answers for? What three things are really kicking the slats out of your life?"

They spent a few minutes writing, then passed the cards up front, and I began reading some. Pretty soon someone said, "That's the kind of thing we ought to be talking about in here." Before long I had a hard time shutting down the discussion.

Once a guy in the class said, "I don't know if this is the place to talk about it…but to be honest with you, my wife and I sat down Thursday night and said that if we can't get our act together, we're going to break up." That's the kind of comment that'll rattle the rafters, all right. Once again our discussion was off and running.

After all, if people can't talk about these things in your Sunday school class and your Bible study group, then where in the world can they talk about them?

Studies have shown, interestingly enough, that there's a direct correlation between *predictability* and *impact*. The higher your predictability, the lower your impact. Conversely, the lower your predictability, the higher your impact. (Please note that this has to do with methodology, not morals.)

The classic illustration is the life of Jesus Christ. They could never figure him out.

One day the Herodians and the Pharisees got together—men who never got together over anything. They wouldn't be caught on the same side of the street, except when they had a common enemy. But because of this trouble-maker Jesus, they convened and said, "Let's hit him with the problem of tax-ation. After all, Herodians are pro-Rome and Pharisees are anti-Rome. So we'll ask him about it. If he says he's for taxation, *we* nail him. If he says he's against it, *you* nail him. Let's go."

They found Jesus and said, "Teacher, should a man pay taxes or not?"

"Got a coin?" Jesus said.

"A coin? Sure, right here." And they passed him a coin.

"Whose inscription is this on it?"

"Ahhh...Caesar's."

"Then render to Caesar the things that are Caesar's, and to God the things that are God's."

Stunned, they left him and quietly regrouped on the sidelines. Finally someone spoke: "Who thought up that dumb question anyway?"

Jesus was far too unpredictable to ever be boring.

It's so painful to go into many of our churches and Sunday school classes and Bible study groups. They're so predictable you can fall asleep, wake up ten minutes later, and find them exactly where you expected them to be.

It's like what the bishop from England said: "You know, wherever the apostle Paul went, they had a riot or a revival. Wherever I go, they serve tea."

And what do they do where you go?

Fighting Silence

Ever looked at your dog's face after you've asked him a serious question? That's the kind of reaction I'll often get in a class when I first ask them some-thing: just those silent puppy dog looks.

So I think, "Maybe they didn't understand it," and I'll rephrase the question—and get the same response. I've actually had someone say to me, "We don't talk in here; you're the pro, you tell us."

So I say, "But you're the pros in living. I have confidence in you, and I expect you to talk in here and tell me what you think. If it's on your mind, then I want to hear it." I ask the question again and say nothing else.

They're dreadfully aware of the silence. A few people will cough. But I'm very patient—I can wait as long as they can.

Finally someone says, "Well, I'll tell you what I think. It may not be right, but I think…" The barrier is broken.

I know from years of observation that the average adult—whether lawyer, pro athlete, factory worker, or whatever (I've taught them all, and it's true for each one)—has a very low level of confidence in his use and understanding of the Scriptures, and therefore a lack of confidence to speak out in class. What can you do about it?

Early in my ministry to the Dallas Cowboys I told them, "Men, we're going to learn how to study the Bible."

Their response was a riot to see—and hear. "Thanks a lot, Doc, but you don't understand," they said. "We're football players." One of the quarterbacks insisted that the linemen couldn't read. But I got them into Scripture and helped them learn what to look for. Each time they found it, no matter how elementary it was, I went through the ceiling with excitement.

That's the key, in fact, to Bible study: Teach people what to look for, and then they can find it.

If people have confidence in you, your task is to use it to help transfer that confidence to themselves. And the more confident they are in you, the greater your potential of building that self-confidence in them.

It isn't easy, because some of these people have been sitting in those seats for years. They've got hardening of the categories.

When people are afraid to participate in class, one of your best approaches is simply to (1) encourage them to participate and (2) affirm them when they do.

Often I say, "You need to understand that the only foolish question in this class is the unasked question. Because it's like an unremoved splinter: It will fester.

"So we don't laugh at any questions or comments here. We take them seriously."

Then when someone makes a contribution, I say, "Fantastic, thank you!" Or, "I think in all the years I've been studying the Bible I've never seen that insight from this passage. That's great, thank you!" Or, "That's one of the most profound questions I've ever heard on this passage." You *celebrate* what they say. Make a hero out of anyone who contributes.

And then someday when someone in your class says, "This is probably a dumb question, but I've been wanting to ask it for a long time…," you've just been paid one of the best compliments possible. You've created an atmosphere in which someone is free to ask what they've been afraid to ask.

Fielding Tough Questions

What do you do if you're asked a question you can't answer?

Your response is important, because the motto for many in the class is "Better to keep your mouth shut and be thought dumb than to open it and remove all doubt." So try saying, "That's a terrific question, thank you! I don't have an answer for that, but I'll try to get you one."

Maybe you can recall a teacher, perhaps in college, who responded to a student's question with a mumbled "Well…whereas…consequently…whereupon…as it were…most scholars would agree…" and so on, and by this time you're thinking, "Now I know he doesn't have the answer."

The greatest professor I ever had was one of the foremost authorities on the New Testament. One day in class a student asked him a question, and he answered, "Young man, that's the most perceptive question I've been asked in thirty-six years of teaching, and I can't give you an answer to it because my answer would be very superficial. But I'll study it and come back to you with an answer. Any other good questions like that?"

So you don't have to pull the wool over anyone's eyes. Never be embarrassed to say, "I don't know."

How about handling questions that are threatening? This is the area of strength, I believe, for those groups who are most effective in reaching the non-Christian: They are comfortable around very threatening questions, and they don't become defensive.

I was once leading a Bible class designed for unbelievers, taking them through the Gospel of Mark, when a guy put up his hand and asked, "Hey, you don't mean you're telling me Jesus Christ is God, are you?"

How would a question like that be treated in the average church? The response is so important. At stake is someone's eternal salvation.

I answered, "Jim, that's an incredible question, right at the heart of the issue here. It really comes to grips with what we're talking about. Did everyone hear what Jim said? Jim, would you mind repeating it?" Interestingly enough, as you continue the discussion after using this approach, a guy like Jim may not even hear the answers that are given, but he picks up unmistakably on your attitude, and you've won him.

Scorch him in his chair, however, and that's the last question he'll ask, and maybe the last time you'll see him in class.

Controlling Discussion Dominators

What do you do if someone is dominating class discussion—as hard to turn off as Niagara Falls?

Let me give you a three-step plan:

First, express appreciation for his contribution. Tell him privately, "I want you to know I deeply appreciate your interest in this class. Man, if I could get everybody in this class as interested as you are, I'd have it made."

Maybe no one's ever told him that before. Most people give him those looks that say, "Why don't you shut up?" Not that he's heeded them, of course, but he has gotten them.

Second, ask him to do you a favor: "Have you noticed that a lot of people in the class don't participate in the discussion? Would you help me get those people into it? Just hold back a little, work with me in this, and let's see if you and I can get the rest of the class as involved as you are." This approach usually has a fascinating effect.

Finally, during class, call on *him* to answer a question. It may be the first time in history that's happened—and it will come through loud and clear that you genuinely appreciate what he has to say.

I did that once to a guy who had been dominating the class, and he was floored. "Oh—you want *me* to answer?" Afterward he told me, "You know, I guess I've been a little obnoxious."

"Really? What gives you that impression?"

"Oh," he said, "people give you messages. But I just want to thank you for wanting to know what I have to say. Nobody's ever done that for me."

So instead of stifling him, I got him on my team.

That's what we want to do. Teaching is fun, if you get the right picture of what you're doing: Win them to your side.

A student once told me he decided he wanted to get married someday. "Well," I said, "that's refreshing," and I thought, "We're making progress here." "Do you know what kind of woman you're looking for?" I asked.

He pulled out three typewritten pages of specifications.

"I see you've thought about this," I said. "You know, I'm writing a book on marriage. Would you mind if I borrowed your list?"

He was nearly dumbfounded. "Oh, no, of course not, Prof! Anything I can do to help you would be fine." I had won him.

Then I looked over his list and asked him one question: "How many of these standards do *you* meet?"

Developing Note Takers

Finally, realize that most people don't know how to take notes in class—or understand the value of it. If you don't believe it, pick up the paper they leave behind after class is over. I do this regularly when I go to a church to speak— a little janitorial work, not a part of the contract, but really interesting for me. If I used an illustration about an Eskimo dog to make a point, I'll find a sheet of paper with the one word "dog" written on it. Perhaps it was written by the same lady who greeted me at the door after the message and said, "You know, I once had an Eskimo dog too."

You can help people become better note takers by providing them with a basic outline of the content for each class. Week by week you can begin making the notes less and less detailed, so they begin to do a little filling in. They'll soon get to the point of not writing down simply "dog" but what the dog illustration is teaching. So you gradually train people to listen intelligently.

I once taught a Bible class in Dallas for professional men, one of whom was a graduate of the Massachusetts Institute of Technology—a man with several advanced degrees, very articulate, and highly sought after as a consultant. He had no lack of mental marbles.

Yet he used to come to our class and sit and listen with his eyes open but his hands folded.

One class night, during a coffee break, I said to him, "I understand you went to MIT."

"That's right."

"Enjoy it?"

"Oh, very stimulating."

"Did you take any notes there?"

"You mean at MIT?"

"Yeah."

"Oh, of course. Reams of them."

"Find them helpful?"

"Oh, very helpful. They're my bread and butter, my lifeline."

"That's great. Did you ever think of taking any notes here?"

"You mean here? Here in the Bible class?"

"Yeah."

"No," he said, "I never thought of that. That's a good idea."

"I thought it was."

The next week he came with a clipboard and took notes. We were scarcely into the hour when he stood up and said, "Hey, Hendricks. I've got a question." And he hasn't stopped asking questions since. Suddenly he was catapulted from the fringe right to the very heart of the learning process. He's learned to relate biblical truth to his profession and to his life, and he's very much alive.

veryone

who is fully trained

will be like his teacher.

LUKE 6:40B

Making the Investment

Now for a final review. To you as a teacher—to stimulate your thinking, to stir your feelings, and to spur you on to action—we've presented in this book seven basic principles, in the form of an acrostic:

T The Law of the Teacher—Stop growing today, and you stop teaching tomorrow.

E The Law of Education—How people learn determines how you teach.

A The Law of Activity—Maximum learning is always the result of maximum involvement.

C The Law of Communication—To truly impart information requires the building of bridges.

H The Law of the Heart—Teaching that impacts is not head to head, but heart to heart.

E The Law of Encouragement—Teaching tends to be most effective when the learner is properly motivated.

R The Law of Readiness—The teaching learning process will be most effective when both student and teacher are adequately prepared.

These "laws" are principles—basic principles woven forever into the fabric of effective teaching. Whatever age group you teach, or whatever subject, or whatever cultural setting you're involved in, your understanding and application of these laws can help you make a permanent difference in the lives of others.

But keep in mind that these really are *only* principles. When it comes to carrying out his purposes, God doesn't use principles; he uses people.

Your success in your calling as an effective teacher depends not on your knowledge of these laws, but on *you* as a person, and most strategically on your openness to God's power in your life. The key is not what you do for

God but what you allow *him* to do through you. God wants to use you as his catalyst—and as you let him transform and renew your thinking, you'll be ready for his use.

Are you, therefore, willing to permit God to change you so you can truly impact others? That willingness—that commitment—could well be the biggest step forward in your success in teaching.

A veteran missionary once described Eastern European Christians as commitment-rich and information-poor, and Western believers as information-rich and commitment-poor. Too many of us in the church in the West are slouching into a deformed, underdeveloped posture because of commitment deficiency.

So the question nags: Are we willing to pay the price for development? There is, after all, a cost involved. Effective teaching isn't available at any bargain-basement sale.

If you have the facts in view, I know you'll go ahead and gladly pay the cost. The thrill and fulfillment of effective teaching is just too satisfying to throw away in favor of limited living and lesser goals.

And as you continue investing your life in others, I trust you'll return to this book as a helpful guide for putting theory into behavior—which is exactly what it's designed to do.

Multnomah Publishers

The publisher and author would love to hear your comments about this book. *Please contact us at:*
www.multnomah.net/teachingtochange

Lesson Plans

Learning is change. And few things facilitate individual change like the accountability of studying with others. The concepts of this book will be better reinforced and incorporated as teachers dialogue and apply these principles with fellow teachers. These lesson plans have been provided to help you lead a group through this process.

The interactive outlines are divided into three sections—the approach, content analysis, and personal application. This format will be used for each of the seven principles.

Approach

The adults coming into your session have lots of things on their minds, much of which has little to do with being a better teacher. The function of this segment is to capture their attention. The activities are to hook them and guide their thoughts towards the topic to be discussed in the Analysis section.

Analysis

The purpose of this part of the session is to further clarify and understand the concepts in the chapter. A variety of methods will be used to explore and gain insights into these principles for effective teaching.

Application

When students understand the conceptual elements of teaching, it's time to move to implications. A response is needed. This segment of the plan will have learners identifying ways they can practice these teaching principles in their own unique ministry contexts.

Lesson 1: The Law of the Teacher

APPROACH

Write the following four statements from Dr. Hendricks on the board. Have each teacher choose the one that is the most meaningful to him or her and write a two-minute lecture, expanding on this concept.

1. "In the search for good teachers, I always look for FAT people—those who are Faithful, Available, and Teachable." (p. 19)

2. "…effective teaching comes only through a changed person. The more you change, the more you become an instrument of change in the lives of others. If you want to become a change agent, you also must change." (pp. 20–21)

3. "The two factors that will influence you the most in the years ahead are the books you read and the people you're around." (p. 26)

4. "Experience does not necessarily make you better; in fact it tends to make you worse, unless it's *evaluated* experience. The good teacher's greatest threat is satisfaction—the failure to keep asking, 'How can I improve?'" (p. 33)

ANALYSIS

Have the class share their lectures in groups of three or four. If you have fewer than six participants, keep them together in one group.

FOR LARGE GROUP DISCUSSION

1. What were some of the interesting insights in the lectures shared?

2. What would you say are some of the most important ways you've grown in your beliefs about and attitudes towards teaching?

3. How do you think a person's spiritual development is affected by his or her growth—or lack of growth—in each of these four areas: physical, intellectual, social, emotional? Are any of these more important than the others? Why?

4. If people cannot develop spiritually unless they develop in the physical, intellectual, social, and emotional dimensions of life, in what ways can we facilitate growth in these crucial areas? Brainstorm on these four dimensions, creating a list on the board of practical ways one can stimulate growth in each of these arenas of life.

 APPLICATION

The unexamined life is not worth living. Nor does the unexamined life produce meaningful personal growth. For change to take place, it necessitates being intentional about the crucial dimensions of our lives.

Have each member of the group fill in the following chart, listing one to three strengths and weaknesses in each of these areas.

LIFE DIMENSIONS	STRENGTHS	WEAKNESSES
PHYSICAL		
INTELLECTUAL		
SOCIAL		
EMOTIONAL		

PLAN OF ACTION

Ask each teacher to write down a plan of action to improve in one of these four areas over the next thirty days. Have them share this with a fellow teacher and commit to asking each other about their progress in working their plans over the next month.

Lesson 2: The Law of Education

APPROACH

Ask each member of the group to take a sheet of paper and create a symbolic drawing on learning. Using stick figures or other designs, they are to illustrate or diagram their thoughts on "How does a person learn?" You may use the illustrations below to get them started, or develop your own.

ANALYSIS

Have each person share his or her drawings with a partner. Listen for ideas and concepts from these drawings on how students learn, and bring these back to discuss with the entire group.

FOR LARGE GROUP DISCUSSION

1. What insights on learning did you discover from the symbolic drawing exercise? (Write these on the board and add to the list during the discussion.)

2. Think back on something you learned over the past year, possibly a piece of knowledge, a new skill, or a change in attitude. What factors helped you in the learning process? What hindered your learning?

3. In the learning process, what is the role of the teacher? The role of the learner? If these roles were fleshed-out in the classroom, what would you see the teacher and learners doing?

4. How does failure fit into one's experience of learning? When has failure been personally helpful to your growth?

FOR SMALL GROUP DISCUSSION

Divide the class into groups of two to four people (organized by ministry areas—teachers of children, youth, and adults), and have them answer the following question about Luke 9:1–17: "If we wish to help our students master the basic skills of reading, writing, listening, and speaking, what kinds of discovery activities could we use to communicate this passage of Scripture?"

 ## APPLICATION

Assign the group to do the following writing exercise individually: Select two students whom you are teaching, and analyze their differences. What seems to be unique about the way they think and learn? How are they different in their understanding of the Bible and their experience level as Christians? What differences are you aware of in their backgrounds—family dynamics, geography, culture, education, economic level, etc.?

Student #1:

Student #2:

In light of this information, how would you approach teaching Luke 9:1–17 to these two students? Over the course of the next few months try to do this exercise for each student in your group.

Lesson 3: The Law of Communication

APPROACH

AGREE–DISAGREE ACTIVITY

Put the following statement on the board or overhead.

> Maximum learning is always the result of maximum student
> involvement, for we always learn by doing.

Have those who "agree" go to one side of the room and those who "disagree" to the opposite side of the room (no "fence straddlers" allowed). Have an informal debate, letting each side try to convince the others of their positions. Individuals may change sides anytime during the discussion by walking to the other side of the room.

ANALYSIS

FOR GENERAL DISCUSSION

There are certain things to keep in mind regarding the Law of Activity. Brainstorm with the class what questions we should ask ourselves as we try to engage our students actively in the learning process. A few ideas are listed to get everyone started:

> Are the activities appropriate for the ages and interests of
> my students?

Does this activity have a planned purpose, or is it just busy-work to occupy time or entertain with no clear objective?

What part does the teacher serve in facilitating this activity?

Can you think of any activities that might get in the way of effective teaching? Discuss them and why they are a hindrance.

Have teachers share their positive experiences of actively involving students in learning activities. What did they learn about the teaching/learning process from these experiences?

CASE STUDY

Divide the class into small groups of three or four. Have each group look at one of the situations below and come up with a list of three or four specific activities (research, crafts, music, art, discussion, creative writing, drama, etc.) to meaningfully involve the students in these passages.

1. You are teaching a group of eight- to ten-year-olds the parable in Mark 4:1–9. What activities would be appropriate and for which part of the lesson (i.e. introduction/hook, Bible exploration, or application section)?

2. Judges 6 has been assigned to your senior-high class, all of whom have studied this story from their childhood days. Identify some learning activities you could use to help them apply this familiar passage to their lives.

3. The lesson aim for Ephesians 2:1–3 is "to define worldliness, listing ways worldliness manifests itself in believers, and to identify one 'weakness of the world' to trust God to work in this week." What activities could you use for teaching this segment of the Word to your Young Marrieds' Class?

 **APPLICATION**

Properly evaluated experience is the best teacher. Ask the teachers to rate themselves on the following "Law of Activity" scale by placing a circle around the number that accurately reflects their experience. Then have them write a plan to improve in *one* area.

LAW OF ACTIVITY SCALE

1 = Always   2 = Usually   3 = Half the Time   4 = Rarely   5 = Never

1. I make an intentional effort not to lecture/tell students those things they could learn better through active self-discovery.	1 2 3 4 5
2. I have a planned objective for using learning activities with my students, not just as entertainment or busywork.	1 2 3 4 5
3. I reflect on how this activity will facilitate learning and help my students to apply Bible truth.	1 2 3 4 5
4. I ask myself if this activity will be too time-consuming or is unrealistic in terms of supplies needed for the task.	1 2 3 4 5
5. I use different types of learning activities in each of my lessons.	1 2 3 4 5
6. I give students a choice of learning activities and freedom in adjusting assignments around their needs.	1 2 3 4 5
7. I seek to increase my personal repertoire of teaching methods and learning activities to use in my classroom teaching.	1 2 3 4 5

Lesson 4: The Law of Communication

Approach

Ask the group to think of a time in the last few months when they felt a strong emotion—anger, joy, sorrow. Take a few minutes to allow everyone to share this personal story with a partner, remembering some of the communication factors presented in this chapter by Dr. Hendricks.

Analysis

After each duo has had a chance to share their stories, transition into the Analysis section by asking people to point out ways their partner effectively communicated through the bridge of the emotional component (such as gestures, facial expressions, tone/varied pitch of voice, etc.).

FOR GENERAL DISCUSSION

1. In your opinion, what kinds of communication "bridges" should be built by the teacher on a one-to-one basis with individual learners and what "bridges" can be built to the class as a whole?

2. Why is it important for your verbal (spoken and written) and nonverbal (body language, actions, and attitudes) communication to be congruent? Can you think of examples when this didn't happen? What were the results?

FOR SMALL GROUPS

Dr. Hendricks provided an example (p. 72) of working through the intellectual, emotional, and volitional components in interacting on what "the Golden Rule means."

Dividing them into ministry groups (children, youth, or adults), have each group try their hand at doing the same process on *one* of the following, selecting either fourth graders or senior saints as their target audience:

1. What does it mean to share your faith with others?

2. What does it mean to experience the power of God (Ephesians 3:14–19)?

What questions could be used in each category of knowing, feeling, and doing for (1) sharing your faith or (2) working through Ephesians 3:14–19? Share the results with the other groups.

PERSONAL REFLECTION

Ask the group to think back over the past few lessons they have taught. What do they think their students saw and heard in regard to the lesson introduction/conclusion; gestures/movement; use of voice; and opportunities for feedback? Ask the teachers to jot down a few notes on how they did in these areas.

BRAINSTORMING EXERCISE

Assign a few of the following areas to each of the small groups. Have them create a list of practical ways teachers can perfect their communication in the following areas:

1. Lesson Introduction

2. Lesson Conclusion

3. Use of Voice

4. Use of Gestures

5. Handling External Distractions

6. Gaining Feedback on Your Teaching

On the board create a list of practical ideas under each category.

 **APPLICATION**

To apply tne concepts of this chapter, have each person check *one* of the following activities to do in the next two weeks

❑ Ask another teacher to observe one o. your class sessions and to give you feedback on a few of the areas from the Brainstorming section.

❑ Have students fill out an anonymous questionnaire— "Letters from Fellow Learners." Ask questions on areas in which you would like feedback, such as:

What do you find enjoyable about our class?

What personal traits of the teacher do you find helpful/distracting?

What do you find boring about our class?

If you could change one thing about our class, what would it be?

❑ Tape record (audio or video) one of your teaching sessions, paying close attention to your lesson's introduction and conclusion. After listening or watching the tape, write out two things you could do to improve your teaching effectiveness.

❑ Observe a teacher who uses his/her voice and gestures effectively. Compare your use of voice and gestures with this teacher, and list a few things you could do to enhance your communication skills.

Lesson 5: The Law of the Heart

Approach

Ask the class to reflect on a positive classroom experience they had when they were the same age at those they teach. What made this class session memorable?

Analysis

Have the group share these classroom experiences in a circle response, and have them listen for what categories these positive elements may fall under:

1. Ethos — the character and credibility of the teacher

2. Pathos — how the teacher aroused passion or touched the emotions

3. Logos — the teacher's logical and thorough command of the content

FOR LARGE GROUP DISCUSSION

1. In your own words, how would you describe "heart-to-heart" teaching?

2. What role does a teacher's vulnerability or self-disclosure play in teaching? In what ways do we need to be cautious about sharing our struggles with our students? What are some practical actions teachers could take to become more vulnerable before their students?

3. Why is it crucial that we "know" our students? What are some ways we could get to know the needs of our students?

"GETTING TO KNOW YOU" PROJECTS

1. Class Survey — Effective teachers get to know their students on a personal level. Divide your class into two groups and have each develop a survey, one for teachers of children and the other for teachers of youth/adults. The surveys might include a few of the following items, but have the groups add their own ideas to this starter list. Have both groups select those that are appropriate for their students and try the survey with their classes.

Name, address, and phone number

School/job responsibilities

Family

Facts about your Christian life

Hobbies and recreational activities

Interests and abilities

Favorite food, vacation spots, etc.

What other things could teachers do to get to know their students better?

2. Top Ten List — Have the teachers create a list of what they think are the top ten needs of their students, placing those needs in order of priority. Then ask your teachers to take an anonymous survey with the individuals in

their class next week, having their students list their top ten needs or concerns, in priority order. Have the teachers compare the students' lists with their own Top Ten lists.

In the next session discuss the following questions: "How well did you know your students?" "How will this information impact your teaching?"

 **APPLICATION**

Wrap up this session by having your teachers do the sentence completion exercises below. Then by triads have them pray for the specific needs of their students.

"The area of ethos, pathos, or logos that I need to work on is..."

"I will do this in the coming weeks by..."

Law 6: The Law of Encouragement

Approach

Ask the teachers to think back to their high school or college days. Which individuals were influential in motivating them? Have the group reflect back on those people and write down what they did that was helpful in motivating them.

Analysis

Create a list on the board or overhead projector of the "Teaching Ministry Motivators" from the Approach Section. Add others to the list that were not expressed by your teachers.

FOR GENERAL DISCUSSION

1. Which of our "Ministry Motivators" were extrinsic? intrinsic?

2. Which type of motivation is more effective in the lives of our students—intrinsic or extrinsic?

3. Are there ways to retool extrinsic motivational methods to make them intrinsic? How?

4. What signals do you look for to know if students in your class are bored?

5. How do you adjust your lesson to refocus their attention?

6. What kind of training series could you structure to encourage people to share their faith, focusing on the stages of telling, showing, and doing?

7. Which of these stages is the most difficult for teachers? Why?

FOR SMALL GROUPS

Divide the class into ministry areas—children, youth, and adult—and have each group come up with some concrete and specific ideas in the following categories that would be useful in a teacher's "Motivational Toolbox."

Ownership —

Curiosity —

Meeting Needs —

Usefulness —

Recognition —

Approval —

Are there other categories you can add to Dr. Hendricks's list?

 APPLICATION

PERSONAL TOOLBOX

Have the teachers take a look at their personal "Motivational Toolbox" and ask themselves:

1. Are there any "rusted tools" that are getting in the way of my students learning and applying the principles taught in my class?

2. What tool is "missing" from my toolbox? What are two specific ways I could be more effective in motivating my students?

Lesson 7: The Law of Readiness

APPROACH

GRAFFITI EXERCISE

As your teachers enter the room, have on the board or on poster board the following, leaving ample space for additional comments:

> LESSON PREPARATION IS... *Full of Stress*
>
> *Exciting*   *Time!!!*   *Wonderfully Creative*
>
> *A Learning Adventure*
>
> *Painful*

Give teachers markers and have them finish the sentence with words or phrases to express their thoughts and feelings about lesson preparation.

ANALYSIS

PANEL INTERVIEW

Select three or four of your more experienced teachers, and interview them in a general panel discussion. You could ask:

What steps do you take in preparing to teach? Which of these steps are the most helpful? the least helpful?

What is the most frustrating aspect to lesson preparation? How do you deal with this challenge?

If you were starting your teaching ministry over again, what things would you do differently in terms of lesson preparation?

If you were giving advice to new teachers, what would you share?

Then open it up for other questions from the floor!

FOR SMALL GROUPS

In ministry groups (children, youth, adult teachers) have them choose *one* of the following three activities:

Assignments — What assignments prior to class could you give your students to prepare them for studying Psalm 23? Be sure they match the criteria presented by Dr. Hendricks.

Questions — Develop six or seven questions on Luke 15:11–32 (the story of the Prodigal Son) that could be used in your class to further explore this parable. Be sure to balance your list with informational, analytical, and applicational types of discussion questions.

Leading Discussions — When you are leading discussions with your class, what can you do when:

No one responds to a question;

Someone monopolizes the discussion;

Comments are irrelevant to the discussion;

Participants disagree;

Someone gives a "wrong" or even heretical answer?

Gather the groups back together and have them share their results.

 **APPLICATION**

Have the teachers develop a plan of action for improving or changing one area of their lesson preparation. Also, ask them to consider establishing a partnership with a fellow teacher to hold each other accountable for "early" preparation. As a part of this, they should agree on an amount of time they feel is adequate for their preparation and when they hope to have their lesson ready. Then partners can consistently pray for and check up on one another.

WRITTEN PRAYERS

Give your teachers 5" x 8" cards and have them write a prayer to God, thanking him for the changes that have taken place in their teaching over the past few months, and also listing one or two areas they would like the Lord's assistance in teaching to change lives.

Close the series by having a time of prayer, allowing individuals to read their cards expressing their thanks to God and their desires to see the Lord at work in the lives of their students.

Transform Your Teaching with "The Seven Laws of the Teacher Seminar" on Video

Let Howard Hendricks and Bruce Wilkinson show you how to revolutionize your communication skills with Walk Thru the Bible's Teacher Training Series.

This book has been developed as part of The Applied Principles of Learning Series™, a unique training curriculum designed to help anyone who wants to be a better communicator, whether as a pastor, Sunday school teacher, Bible study leader, counselor, or parent.

Walk Thru the Bible Ministries has brought together the creative forces of Dr. Howard Hendricks and Bruce H. Wilkinson, founder and president of Walk Thru the Bible, to help you master the secrets of fruitful teaching. Both men are appreciated around the country for their life-changing teaching.

Dr. Hendricks's series, "The Seven Laws of the Teacher," focuses on the seven principles he describes in this book. His videotaped sessions, along with a student notebook and leader's guide, are available for use in churches, schools, or other groups. Bruce Wilkinson's series, "The Seven Laws of the Learner," also is offered on video with accompanying student notebook, leader's guide, and textbook.

From their years of practical experience and insight, these two master communicators have developed this unique seminar to help you increase your skills in order to teach with excellence. For more information about how you can order the video series and materials which accompany this book, contact:

Video Division
Walk Thru the Bible Ministries, Inc.
4201 N. Peachtree Rd.
P.O. Box 80587
Atlanta, Georgia 30366

Phone 1-800-763-5433

RAISE THE STANDARD FOR THE MEN OF AMERICA

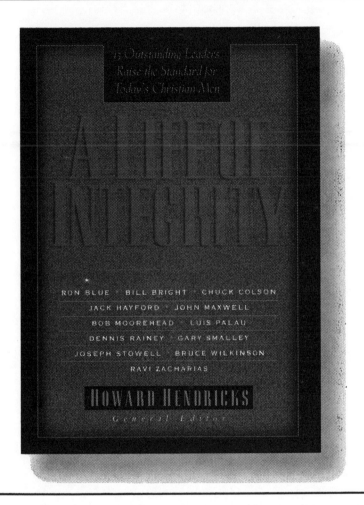

For the first time, thirteen of the most inspirational Promise Keepers speeches ever given are featured together in one volume: *A Life of Integrity*. This unique compilation features favorite messages by many of the most effective Christian leaders and communicators of our day. These are the messages that helped launch the Promise Keepers movement and raise the standard for men across our nation. These are the messages that caused men to cheer and applaud...then fall to their knees and weep. These are the messages that inspired countless numbers of men to dedicate their lives to God and to serve Him with all their hearts.

ISBN 1-57673-136-7